CLOWNS

NERINA ROBERTS

• • •

δελος

CAPE TOWN

© 1991 Delos, 40 Heerengracht, Cape Town

Also available in Afrikaans as *Narre*

Photography by Graham New
Illustrations by Frederick Roberts
Cover design and typography by Debbie Odendaal
Typeset in 10 on 12 pt Century ITC Book by Unifoto, Cape Town
Printed and bound by Printkor, Cape Town

First edition, first impression 1991

ISBN 1-86826-189-1

CONTENTS

• • •

INTRODUCTION

◆ ◆ ◆

Roll up, roll up! Step right this way, ladies. Don't miss the greatest show of cloth clowns ever, yours to make with only the minimum of effort and to enjoy for ever.

Presenting Blinky, a daring young clown on his flying trapeze; Amadeus and his hat full of tricks; Charlie the tramp; Shorty the juggler and many, many more.

Clowns shares with you a selection of carefully designed, full-size patterns for these clowns, their clothes and accessories. The faces, hairstyles and many of the clothes are interchangeable and there are dozens of ideas to copy. No two clowns need ever look the same.

Clowns are for everyone. This is an ideal opportunity to let your imagination run riot. Allow yourself the pleasure of participating in this wonderfully creative hobby. Nothing could be more fun to make than a cloth clown.

EQUIPMENT AND MATERIALS

(*see* Buyer's guide, p. 56)

◆ ◆ ◆

Cloth doll-making does not require much initial outlay as most people already have the basic equipment and material at hand.

Sewing machine

The simplest sewing machine may be used, provided it is in good working order.

Body fabric

Cloth dolls are always better when made from a cotton knit fabric. Buy a good quality fabric with a selvedge-to-selvedge stretch. Be sure that the fabric is colour fast and will not ladder.

Stuffing

Always use a good quality acrylic stuffing to ensure that the doll has a smooth finish and is light and washable.

Air-soluble pen

Obtainable from sewing shops. This pen may be used for marking the fabric – the marks will disappear after several hours or when water is applied.

Sculpture needle

While not essential, this can be a very useful item. A long darner may sometimes be used, but ideally the needle should be thin and about 10 cm long.

Stuffing sticks

A selection of small sticks, chopsticks or crochet hooks, used to push the stuffing into awkward areas such as fingers.

Fabric paints

Most fabric paints are suitable but it is better to use a fairly liquid paint and fine brushes.

Nylon fur/wool

Long-pile nylon fur or chunky wool is used for the hair.

Shoes

Felt is easy to work with but does not wash well. Try feather leather, vinyl, suede or fabric which has been stiffened with iron-on Vilene.

Clothes

A well-stocked sewing basket and plenty of oddments of colourful fabric, buttons, bows, baubles or bells are all you need. As the amount of fabric needed for each garment is so small, exact requirements have not been specified.

DESCRIPTION OF THE CLOWNS
•••

PUDDYSTIX

Just 35 cm tall, this delightful cloth clown is very quick and easy to make. Inexpensive too, as this is the ideal toy for using up oddments of available fabric. By varying the doll's face and hair colour, trimmings and body fabrics, an endless variety of cloth clowns is available from one pattern.

FLOPPY

The aptly named and flexible Floppy is soft, light and can bend and flop in all directions. He is about 55 cm tall and, dressed in colourful clothes, is bound to make anybody happy. All these dolls are made from the same basic pattern – a change of hairstyle, clothing and facial expression makes each one unique. Wearing: (f.l.t.r.) tunic with frills, shoes, hat; tunic, shoes, hat; knee-length tunic, shoes, hat; tunic, shoes, hat.

(standing) **SHORTY AND LITTLE TOT** _(in hoops)_

Shorty is an adorable clown to brighten someone's life. Notice how a change of face and hairstyle will make the clowns look quite different. At 18 cm tall, Little Tot is a miniature version of Floppy. With bells for hands and bows for toes, this tiny clown would make a lovely mobile. Shorty is wearing an all-in-one suit which looks like shirt and knee-length trousers, shoes and hat. Little Tot is wearing an all-in-one tunic.

8

(left) *AMADEUS AND CHARLIE* (right)

One of the larger clowns in the book, Amadeus measures 75 cm from the top of his hat to the tip of his shoes. Amadeus will gladden any heart with his hat full of tricks. Charlie is made from the same pattern as Amadeus and therefore just as large. This delightful tramp with his beard and braces is intended as an ornament. Amadeus is wearing a coat, shirt, tie, trousers, shoes and top hat. Charlie is wearing a shirt, trousers, shoes and hat.

BLINKY
_____

Blinky is 55 cm tall and the ideal toy clown – happy, cuddly and soft. Dress him in colourful clothes and present him to someone special. He is wearing colourful dungarees, shirt and shoes.

P O C K E T S

Pockets is everyone's favourite. At 55 cm tall and with a smiling face, his appearance can be changed by simply mixing and matching his wardrobe. He is wearing a jacket, waistcoat, trousers, shoes and hat.

GENERAL INSTRUCTIONS
•••

Preparing the pattern and cutting out the clown

The patterns are all actual size. Trace the pattern pieces on to a firm piece of cardboard, transferring all the details. Cardboard is used as it will prolong the life of the traced pattern and it is easier to draw around. Cut out all the pieces and punch a small hole in each. After use, the patterns may be threaded on to a pipe-cleaner for safe storage (see dia. 1).

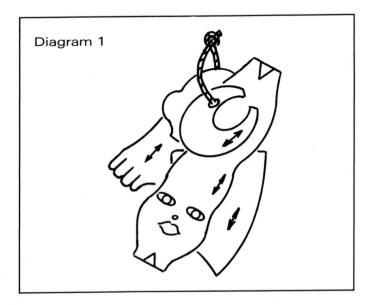

Diagram 1

Select all the pieces needed to make the clown of your choice. Double the body fabric with the selvedges together and place on a cutting board or a table. Place the cardboard pattern in position, ensuring that all the arrows go in the correct direction (see dia. 2). Beware of turning one or more pieces incorrectly in order to save material (see dia. 3). This may result in the clown having, for example, one short, fat arm and one long, thin arm or the clothes may not fit.

Draw around each piece with an air-soluable pen. Remove the cardboard and return the pattern pieces to the pipe-cleaner. Carefully cut out all the pieces of the clown except the arms and, where applicable, the ears. These are easier to sew before cutting out and at this stage are cut out roughly.

Painting the face

If you are an experienced artist, you may wish to leave the painting of the face until after the clown has been completed. In this way you will ensure that the features

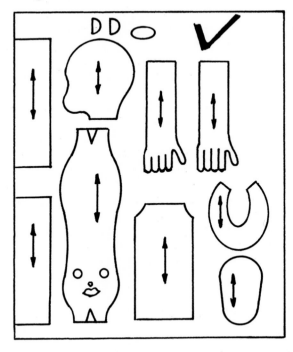

Diagram 2

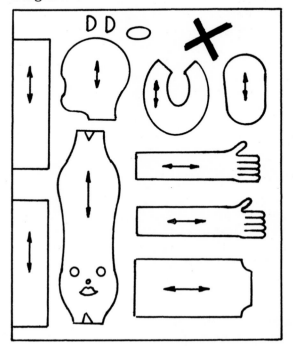

Diagram 3

are in exactly the correct position and you will have the advantage of selecting a face to suit the completed clown.

For the less talented, now is the time to try your hand at painting. If your first attempt is not successful, you will only have wasted a small portion of fabric. Try again and again, if necessary. Painting the faces takes practise but is well worth the effort. Luckily with clowns, small errors can easily be disguised by adding extra facial decoration such as a stripe or a star.

Most fabric paints will do but liquid paints give the best results. Shake the bottle well and often or else the paint may become thin and could bleed into the fabric. Fabric pens work well but should also be tested to ensure that they do not bleed.

Buy good quality brushes in several sizes. A size 2 is best for the large areas. Sizes 00 and 000 are needed for the finer lines. Needless to say, the brushes must be kept scrupulously clean. The golden rule for painting is: be patient and always allow one coat to dry completely before proceeding to the next.

If painting is not for you, choose a face that can be cut from felt. You may, of course, embroider the face if you prefer. This is best done after the clown has been stuffed.

Sewing instructions

The actual clowns need to be sewn very well as a lot of stress is placed on the seams during the stuffing. The clowns that have been designed for play will also have to endure rough handling.

It is advisable to sew the clowns by machine. Use a stretch stitch or a small zigzag for sewing all the seams. If the machine does not have either of these stitches, a straight stitch may be used but all seams must be sewn twice.

An average size stitch will be fine but smaller stitches must be used around the tiny curves of the finger tips. If you are forced to hand-sew, it is essential to use a back-stitch and very strong thread. Sew right sides together, unless otherwise stated, and keep the seams as narrow as possible, no more than 4 mm.

Stuffing the clown

Correct stuffing is probably the most important part of cloth dollmaking. No matter how beautiful the costume or how artistically the face is painted, an incorrectly stuffed doll will never look right. Ensure that the dolls are stuffed hard. The large clowns will need at least 500 g of stuffing each.

Head/body

With clowns it may be alright to stuff the legs and arms a little softer but the head/body section must always be stuffed hard. Use large pieces of stuffing and feed the stuffing into the head.

Using your hands, push the stuffing up against the crown of the head. Continue feeding the stuffing into the head until it is very hard. Remember that when you are working with a stretch fabric, it is very important that you do not allow the head to become bigger and bigger.

Squeeze, mould and pat the head while you work to ensure that the stuffing is compacted and that the head retains a good shape. Continue in this manner until the body is also firmly stuffed. The neck should have no wobble whatsoever, but it is also important not to over-stuff the neck or it will be too fat and the clothes will not fit. Try compacting the stuffing by strangling the doll. It might sound terrible but it works well!

Arms/legs

Using a small stick, push tiny pieces of stuffing into each finger. Use two or three pieces per finger. Continue stuffing the arms, once again squeezing to compact the stuffing.

Stuff the feet firmly. Pound them on the table or on the palm of your hand to keep the soles flat. Continue stuffing the legs. Pull and squeeze them while you work to retain a good shape.

After stuffing, the openings may be sewn closed using a ladder stitch (see dia. 4).

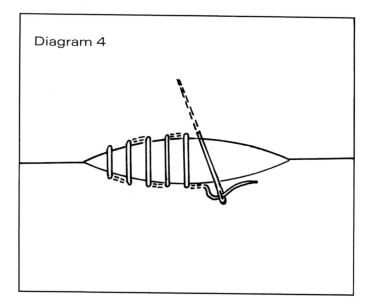

Diagram 4

INSTRUCTIONS FOR SMALLER CLOWNS

• • •

PUDDYSTIX

Just 35 cm tall, this delightful cloth clown is very quick and easy to make. Inexpensive too, as this is the ideal toy for using up oddments of available fabric. By varying the doll's hairstyle, trimmings and body fabrics, an endless variety of cloth clowns is available from one pattern.

Instructions

1. Cut out all the necessary pieces following the instructions on the pattern.
2. Begin with the front. Pin one head-, two hand- and two shoe-sections to the neck, arms and legs respectively. Sew as indicated on dia. 5. Repeat for the back. Press each side neatly so that the head, hands and shoes are in their correct positions.

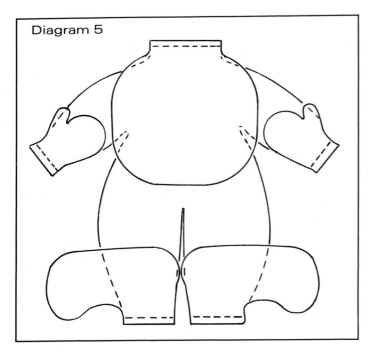

Diagram 5

3. Trace the face on to the head and paint it using the colours of your choice. Allow to dry.
4. With right sides together, sew the back to the front right round, leaving an opening as shown on the pattern. Turn to the right side.
5. Stuff the doll firmly and sew closed.
6. The hair: wind thick wool about six times around three or four of your fingers. Holding all the loops together, sew in a bunch to the head, using a strong matching thread and not the same wool. Make lots of these bunches of 'hair' and sew them all over the head until the entire crown is covered. Cut the loops and trim the hair. (See dia. 6.)

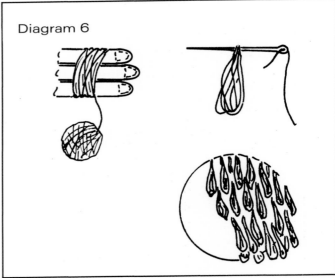

Diagram 6

7. Sew two buttons to the front of the tunic/body and a pom-pom on each shoe. Gather ribbon around the neck or tie a big bow.

FLOPPY AND LITTLE TOT

The aptly named and flexible Floppy is soft, light and can bend and flop in all directions. He is around 55 cm tall and, dressed in colourful clothes, is bound to make anybody happy. At 18 cm tall, Little Tot is a miniature version of Floppy. With bells for hands and bows for toes, these tiny clowns would make a lovely mobile.

FLOPPY

If desired, this clown can easily be made smaller. Leave the head/body the same size. Cut a few centimetres off the arms and legs and remember to adjust the tunic accordingly.

Instructions

As this doll is so simple to make, any fabric may be used although it is always easier to work with cotton knit.

HEAD/BODY (see dia. 7)

1. Cut a rectangle of fabric 35 cm long × 30 cm wide for the head/body.
2. Fold in half lengthwise with the right side of the fabric to the inside. Sew the long side as shown on the diagram.
3. Gather around one end of the tube and pull up tightly.
4. Turn to the right side and stuff. Sew closed, with the seam to the back of the body.
5. Tie string tightly around the doll, about 15 cm down from the gathers, to form the neck.

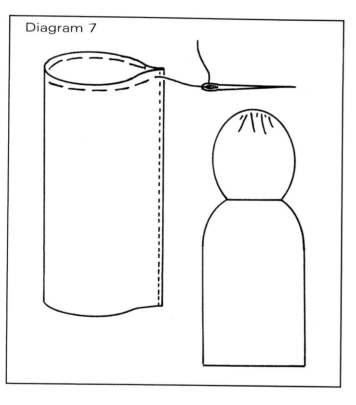

Diagram 7

ARMS (see dia. 8)

1. Cut out the arms following the instructions on the pattern.
2. Two pattern pieces will form one arm. With right sides together, sew around the outside, leaving the tops open for stuffing.
3. Turn to the right side and stuff half of each arm. Machine sew across each arm above the stuffing. Complete the stuffing and sew closed.
4. Sew the arms to the sides of the body by hand, about 3 cm down from the neck.

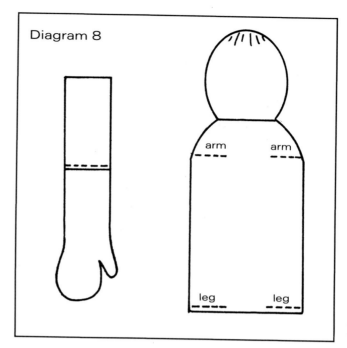

Diagram 8

LEGS/SHOES (see dia. 9)

1. Cut out two large shoe uppers and two large soles, following the instructions on the pattern. Add trimming to the shoe uppers.
2. Cut two rectangles of fabric each 30 cm long × 17 cm wide for the legs.
3. Sew each lower leg to a shoe upper A to B to A.
4. Fold lengthwise and sew the back seams of the legs/shoe uppers.
5. Sew on the soles. Turn to the right side.
6. Stuff the shoe and half of each leg. Machine sew across each leg as for the arms. Complete the stuffing and sew closed, gathering the tops of the legs slightly.
7. Sew the legs to the lower body by hand.

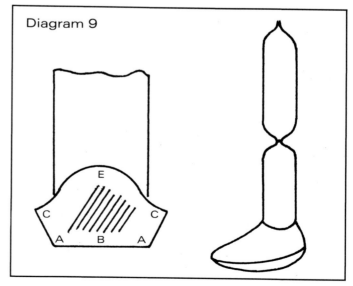

Diagram 9

15

FACE

The faces supplied for Floppy are actual size and very simple. They may be painted, cut from felt or embroidered, using the colours of your choice.

PLASTIC EYES WITH LIDS (see dia. 10)

1. Use either 18 mm wiggly plastic eyes or shank buttons.
2. With strong thread and a long needle, enter anywhere at the back of the head and bring the needle out at the eye position.
3. Pull the needle through the eye shank and return through the same eye position to the back of the head. Pull the thread tightly and tie off. Repeat for the other eye.
4. Fold the lids in half and gather the curved edges.
5. Place a lid over each eye in the required position and, tucking the gathers behind the eyes, pull up tightly and fasten off.
6. Using a toothpick, put a drop of glue behind each eye to secure the lid.

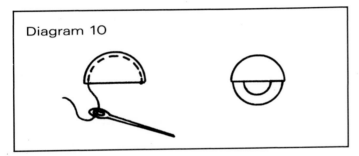

Diagram 10

NOSE (see dia. 11)

1. Cut out the nose of your choice, Using red fabric.
2. Gather around the outer edge.
3. Put a small ball of stuffing in the centre and pull up the gathers tightly.
4. Sew the nose to the face by hand.

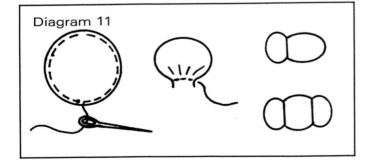

Diagram 11

HAIR

Any of the hairstyles shown in the book may be used.

TUNIC

Instructions (see dia. 12)

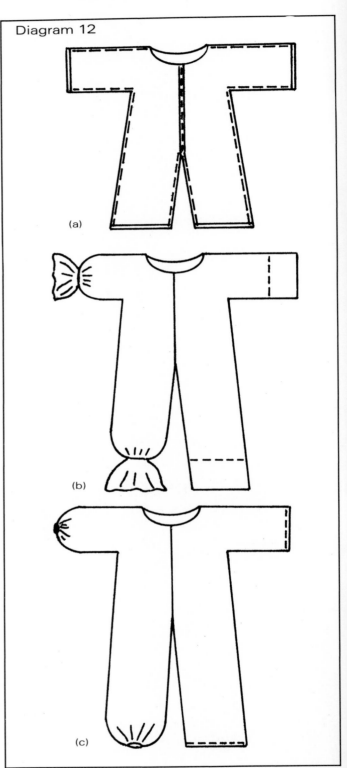

Diagram 12

(a)

(b)

(c)

KNEE-LENGTH TUNIC (a)

This garment is removable.

16

1. Cut out the tunic the same size as the pattern.
2. With right sides together and using two pieces for each half of the garment, sew the tunic along the shoulders, under the arms and down the side and inner leg seams. Join the two halves of the tunic together down the centre front and back seams.
3. Hem the lower leg and the lower sleeve edges. Bind the neck making sure that the opening is large enough to accommodate the doll. If not, make a small opening at the back of the tunic and add a press stud.
4. Turn garment to the right side and press.

FULL-LENGTH TUNIC WITH FRILL (b)

This garment is removable.

1. Cut the legs of the tunic 12 cm and the sleeves 4 cm longer than the pattern.
2. Repeat step 2 as for knee-length tunic.
3. Fold back 4 cm on each sleeve and each leg edge.
4. Stretch and sew elastic along the folded raw edges to gather and form the mock frills.
5. Gather the neck with elastic, turning in the raw edge at the same time.

FULL-LENGTH TUNIC WITH LOOSE CONTRASTING FRILLS (c)

This garment is not removable.

1. Cut out the tunic 8 cm longer than the pattern at the legs only.
2. Repeat step 2 as for knee-length tunic.
3. Turn garment to the right side, press and place the tunic on the doll.
4. Gather the neck, lower sleeve and lower leg edges by hand using a strong thread, folding in the raw edges at the same time. Pull each thread up tightly and fasten off.

FRILLS

1. Cut a strip of fabric 90 cm × 10 cm for the neck frill. Cut four strips of fabric each 50 cm × 6 cm for the arm and leg frills (optional). These sizes are approximate only and the frills may be cut to any suitable size in accordance with the trimming used.
2. Hem and trim one long edge of each frill. Form circles by sewing the short ends of each frill together.
3. Place the frills around the neck, ankles and wrists with the hemmed edge to the outside. Gather the inner edges, folding in the raw edge at the same time. Pull up tightly and fasten off.

HATS AND OTHER TRIMMINGS (see p. 24 and p. 26)

LITTLE TOT

Instructions for doll (see dia. 7)

1. Cut a rectangle of fabric 10 cm × 13 cm for the head/body.
2. Fold in half lengthwise with the right side of the fabric to the inside. Sew one long and one short side.
3. Turn to the right side and stuff lightly. Sew closed.
4. Tie thread tightly around the doll about 5 cm down for the neck.
5. Cut two rectangles of fabric each 4 cm × 6 cm for the arms. Cut two rectangles of fabric each 6 cm × 11 cm for the legs.
6. Repeat steps 2 and 3 above as for the head/body.
7. Sew the arms and the legs to the body.
8. Sew tiny tufts of wool to the forehead and to the sides of the face.
9. Paint a simple face.

Instructions for clothes

HAT

1. Cut a rectangle of suitable fabric 12 cm × 10 cm. Fold in half lengthwise with the right side of the fabric to the inside (6 cm × 10 cm).
2. Sew the long side. Turn to the right side. Press.
3. Sew the hat to the doll's head tucking in the raw edge at the same time.
4. Gather the opposite edge, tucking in the raw edge at the same time and add a small bell.

TUNIC

1. Cut out the tunic following the instructions on the pattern.
2. With right sides together, sew the two pieces of the tunic together along the shoulders, under the arms and down the side and the inner leg seams. Turn garment to the right side.
3. Press and place the tunic on the doll.
4. Gather the wrists tightly, tucking in the raw edges at the same time. Add a small bell for each hand.
5. Gather the neck tightly, tucking in the raw edge at the same time. Add a small ribbon neck frill (see Frills on p. 27 for method).
6. Repeat the gathering at the ends of the legs but leave 1 cm of each leg protruding for the foot. Add a small bow to each foot.
7. Sew two tiny bows to the front of the tunic.

CANE RING (see p. 27)

Pose the little clown in the ring and stitch into place.

INSTRUCTIONS FOR LARGER CLOWNS

• • •

Amadeus, Charlie, Blinky, Pockets and Shorty are all made in the same way. The larger clowns (Amadeus, Charlie) will require about 50 cm of cotton knit fabric and the smaller clowns (Blinky, Shorty and Pockets) will need 30 cm each. Use a ball needle in the sewing machine as it will slide between the threads of the fabric and prevent possible ladders. Keep the seams as narrow as possible.

1. Begin by tracing and cutting out the paper pattern pieces or use your cardboard patterns.

2. Pin the paper pattern pieces onto the fabric to be used for the body, ensuring that the arrows follow the direction of the least stretch.

3. Using an air-soluble pen, draw around each piece. It is not necessary to reverse any of the pieces.

4. Cut out all the pieces on the line except the arms and, where applicable, the ears, following the instructions on the pattern. It is easier to sew the arms and the ears on the actual line and the pattern has been designed accordingly. Cut out roughly around each piece for the time being.

5. ***Painting the face***
   ■ Place the fabric centre head panel on top of the pattern of the chosen face and trace. Hold up to the light or against a window, if necessary. Use either an air-soluble pen or a very light pencil.
   ■ Paint the face according to the instructions on the pattern. Allow each coat of paint to dry before proceeding to the next. When completely dry, outline all the features in black.

6. ***Head and body*** (*see dia. 13*)
   ■ Sew the chin and back-of-head darts in the centre head panel.
   ■ Sew the centre head panel to the head sides A to B. Set aside.
   ■ Sew the body at the shoulders and down the sides. Leave the bottom edge open.
   ■ To attach the head to the body, turn the head to the right side. Leave the body on the wrong side. Put the head inside the body at the neck. Match the chin dart to the centre front of the body. Match the back-of-head dart to the centre back of the body. Sew right round. Turn to the right side.

■ Stuff the head and body firmly, taking care not to stretch the doll out of shape, particularly at the neck. Sew closed.

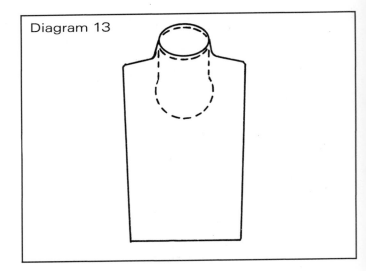

Diagram 13

7. ***Arms*** (*see dia. 14*)
   ■ Sew around the arms on the line, leaving the tops open as shown. Cut out and turn to the right side.
   ■ Sew in the finger-dividing lines.
   ■ Stuff firmly, pushing tiny pieces of stuffing down into each finger tip with the aid of a small stick. Use larger pieces of stuffing for the hands and arms. For arms that can bend, follow step 3 for Floppy's arms and refer to dia. 8.
   ■ Sew the tops of the arms closed and stitch the arms to the body by hand where indicated.

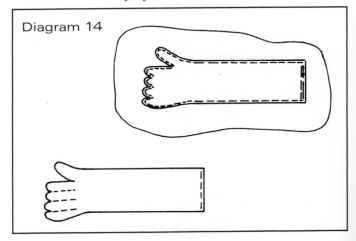

Diagram 14

8. **Shoes and legs** *(see dia. 9)*

The shoes form the feet. Use either the large feet as shown on Floppy and Charlie or the smaller feet belonging to Blinky, Pockets and Shorty. For loose shoes such as the tennis shoes on Amadeus and Shorty, make the smaller feet from the same fabric as the body. See separate instructions for trimming the shoes.

■ Sew the trimmed upper shoes to the lower legs from A along to B along to A.

■ Sew the back seams of the legs from C up to A up to D.

■ Sew on the soles. Stuff firmly. For legs that can bend, follow step 6 for Floppy's legs and refer to dia. 9.

■ Sew the tops of the legs closed and sew the legs to the body by hand.

9. **Toes** *(for Charlie only)*

■ Trace the toes onto the body fabric, following the instructions on the pattern.

■ Sew right round the curved edges. Cut out and turn to the right side.

■ Stuff the toes firmly, pushing tiny pieces of stuffing into each toe with the aid of a small stick. Sew closed.

■ Cut slits in the shoe uppers and insert the toes.

■ Stitch the toes to the shoes all round to prevent the stuffing from escaping the shoes.

■ Paint the toe nails, making sure their edges appear dirty.

10. **Nose — use red fabric, preferably cotton knit** *(see dia. 11)*

■ Follow the instructions for Floppy's nose OR

■ Repeat steps 1 to 3 for Floppy's nose. Now wind thread around one section of the nose to form a nostril. Repeat for the other nostril.

■ Sew the nose to the face by hand.

11. **Ears** *(see dia. 15)*

Make two ears for each clown. Cut them out roughly at the pattern stage.

■ Sew right round the ears, leaving the straight side open. Cut out and turn to the right side.

■ Top stitch along the solid line.

■ Pin the ears to the side of the head, facing forward. Sew to the head by hand, tucking in the raw edges at the same time.

■ The ears may be folded back and secured with a small stitch. Charlie's ears are sewn on top of the hair.

12. **Hair**

Choose the hairstyle you feel best suits your clown.

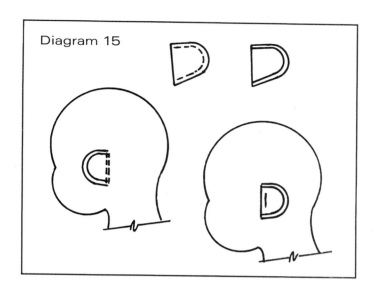

Diagram 15

Hairstyles

WOOL

Finding the right wool for the hair is never a problem. There are so many interesting yarns available that even the simplest hairdo can look stunning. Choose anything from the chunky multi-coloured acrylic used for Puddy-stix to the fine thread used for the glitzy Floppy.

1. **As shown on Pockets** *(see dia. 16)*

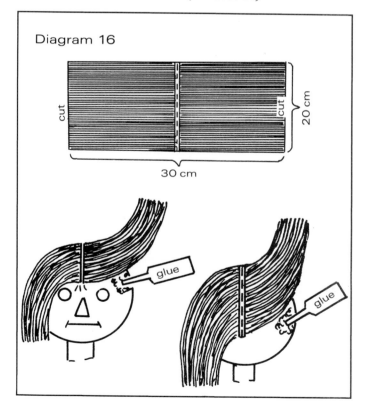

Diagram 16

cut   cut   20 cm

30 cm

glue

glue

- Cut many strands of wool, each about 30 cm long.
- Lay the strands down side by side and put sticky tape across the centre.
- Sew through the centre of the tape which must then be removed.
- Place the wig onto the doll's head so that the sewing forms the centre parting. Sew the wig to the head along this parting.
- Lift half the hair and cover the head underneath with glue. Repeat for the other side.
- Allow the hair to drop down casually onto the glue and trim into a shaggy style.

2. **As shown on Shorty** (*see dia. 17*)
- Take two contrasting strands of wool and make a string of loops about two metres long. This may be done by winding wool around a 2-metre long strip of thin cardboard (width about 16 cm).
- Machine sew along the centre of this strip and break away the cardboard.
- Starting at the hairline, sew the string of loops round and round the head until the entire crown is covered.

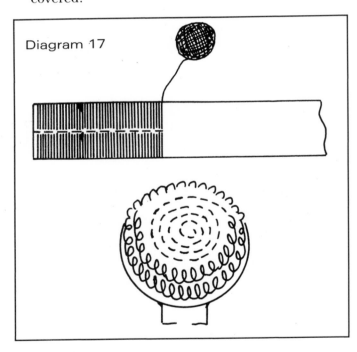

Diagram 17

3. **As shown on Shorty** (*see dia. 6*)
- Sew the jelly bag to the head and make hair for the forehead only OR make the hat removable and cover the entire crown with hair.
- Follow the instructions for Puddystix' hair but make the loops very short by winding the wool around one finger only.

4. **As shown on Floppy** (*see dia. 6*)
- Follow the instructions for Puddystix' hair but

make the loops much longer. Use a piece of cardboard about 6 or 8 cm wide if the loops formed around four fingers don't appear long enough.
- After all the loops have been securely stitched to the crown of the head, cut them and unravel each strand of wool to obtain the curly effect. Be warned that this is a very time-consuming job.

WIGS MADE FROM NYLON CRAFT FUR

1. **As shown on Floppy** (*see dia. 18*)
- Draw a circle on the back of the fur fabric using a plate or bowl about 20 cm in diameter.
- Cut out the circle taking great care not to cut the pile.
- Place the fur onto the doll's head with the right side (fur) against the head, and pin small darts right round until the fur fits the head like a cap. Remove the 'cap' from the head.
- Sew in the darts and cut away the excess fabric. Turn to the right side.
- Sew the wig to the doll's head, right side (fur) up. Brush and trim as desired.

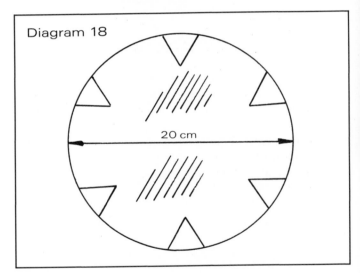

Diagram 18

20 cm

2. **As shown on Amadeus and Charlie**
- Cut a strip of fur 30 cm long × 7 cm wide. Be sure the pile runs in the same direction as the width.
- Sew the strip around the head, folding in the raw edges at the same time. The top of the head is left bald.
- Cut Charlie's beard from the pattern, using the same fur fabric.
- Stitch the beard around the chin just below the mouth.

3. **As shown on Blinky**
Blinky is wearing a wig. These wigs and others are readily available but can be rather expensive.

INSTRUCTIONS FOR MAKING CLOTHES

❖ ❖ ❖

Although the clothes have been designed to be loose fitting, it is nevertheless advisable to fit all the garments as you work, as cloth dolls differ in size depending on how they are stuffed and the type of fabric used for the body.

Most of the clothes are interchangeable and the clowns need not be dressed as shown in the photographs. Decide which clothes you want your clown to wear and then study the patterns and instructions carefully. Most of the necessary adjustments have been given and, with a few additional changes, the clowns can have an endless variety of outfits.

Keep the clothes bright and colourful. Remember to change back to a normal sewing machine needle. *Always* sew the clothes with *right sides together unless otherwise instructed*. A seam measurement of 4 mm has been allowed.

Examples of a mix-and-match wardrobe: Blinky, Pockets and Shorty have the same size head, arms and body width which makes the sun hat, cone hat and jelly bag suitable for all three clowns. Both the small shirt and the waistcoat will also fit these three dolls as will the all-in-one suit, trousers and dungarees which will only need an adjustment by you at the lower legs.

The same jacket is used for Pockets and Amadeus. The pattern shows the adjustments needed - a simple case of altering the length of the sleeves and the lower edge of the jacket.

Jacket *(see dia. 19)*

1. Having cut out the relevant pattern pieces, hem across the top edge of each pocket. Fold in the remaining three sides. Place the pockets in position on the jacket fronts and sew into place.
2. Sew the front linings to the jacket fronts along the opening edge (see dia. 19a). Turn and press so that the front overlaps the lining by 1 cm.
3. Turn back again, right sides together, and sew the front and the lining together at the neck edge. Turn and press.
4. Sew the back to the fronts at the shoulders.
5. To form the collar, sew the sides and the outer edge of the two collar pieces together (see diag. 19b). Turn and press.
6. Sew the open edge of the collar to the wrong side of the neck edge (see dia. 19c). Fold over to the right side and press.

7. Sew the curved edge of each sleeve into an armhole.
8. Sew the underarm and side seams.
9. To form the cuffs: fold line C up onto line D. Press, folding the shaded area to the wrong side. Hem by hand (see dia. 19d).
10. Hem the bottom of the jacket. Sew on the buttons.

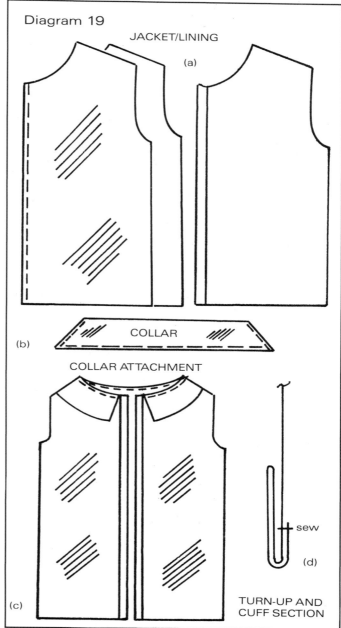

Diagram 19

JACKET/LINING (a)

COLLAR (b)

COLLAR ATTACHMENT

sew (d)

(c)

TURN-UP AND CUFF SECTION

Trousers *(see dia. 20)*

N.B. All side seams are on the fold unless otherwise stated.

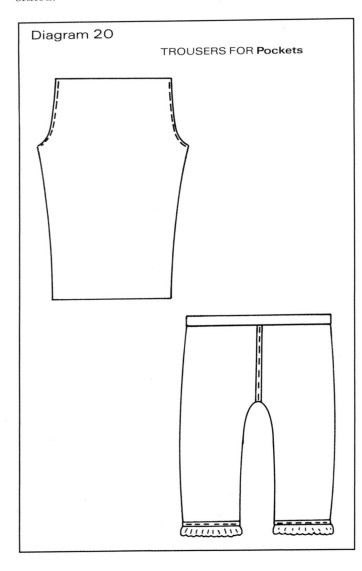

Diagram 20

TROUSERS FOR **Pockets**

POCKETS/SHORTY

1. Cut out the trousers following the instructions on the pattern.
2. Sew the centre back and the centre front seams.
3. Turn the waist edge to the inside and hem to form a casing, tucking in the raw edge at the same time and leave a small section unstitched.
4. Thread elastic through the casing to fit the doll's waist.
5. Sew the ends of the elastic together and sew the small opening closed.
6. Make a narrow hem at the bottom of each leg.
7. Stretch and sew elastic to gather the lower legs.
8. Sew the inner leg seams.
9. Shorty only: Sew on buttons for the braces.

CHARLIE

1. Repeat steps 1, 2 and 8 as for Pockets/Shorty.
2. Sew two rows of top-stitching to form a mock fly on the front left-hand side of the trousers (see dia. 21).
3. Add a few patches, tears, stains and fade marks. For the stains use wax crayons; household bleach can be used to make the fade marks. Sew a few rags to the waist at one side.
4. Sew on the buttons for the braces.

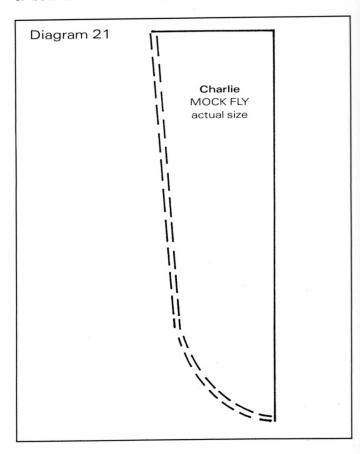

Diagram 21

Charlie
MOCK FLY
actual size

AMADEUS

1. Appliqué the flower onto the pocket and sew the pocket to the trouser leg.
2. Sew the centre back and the centre front seams.
3. Sew the inner leg seams.
4. Make the turn-ups as directed for the jacket cuffs.
5. Fold about 1 cm around the waist to the wrong side and press.
6. Sew on the buttons for the braces.

BLINKY *(dungarees)*

1. Cut out the dungarees following the instructions on the pattern.
2. Sew on a pocket (optional).
3. Sew the centre back and the centre front seams.

4. Sew the inner leg seams.
5. Bind the neck, shoulders and armholes with bias binding.
6. Sew a press stud at each shoulder and two buttons on the front.
7. Measure and hem the lower legs or roll them up.

SHORTY (all-in-one suit)

(Three pattern pieces supplied – trousers, bodice and sleeves)

1. Cut out the pieces following the instructions on the pattern. Note that on the trousers pattern the side seams, which are normally cut on the fold, must be left open and that a small section must be cut away for the armholes.
2. Hem across the top edge of the pocket. Fold in the remaining three sides. Place the pocket in position and sew into place.
3. Sew the centre front seam of the trousers. Sew the lower portion of the centre back seam of the trousers but leave the upper portion open to form part of the back opening.
4. Trim, hem and gather the lower legs.
5. Sew the inner leg seams.
6. Using fabric, ribbon or felt, make two straps each 13 cm × 2 cm.
7. Gather the front and the back two sections of the trousers to fit the bodice front and backs respectively.
8. Sew the bodice backs and front together at the shoulders.
9. Sew the bodice front to the trouser front, catching in the straps on either side at the same time. Repeat for the backs.
10. Trim, hem and gather the lower sleeves.
11. Gather the upper sleeves to fit the armholes. Sew into position.
12. Sew the sleeve seams and down the sides of the bodice/trousers.
13. Make a narrow hem at the neck and down the back opening.
14. Sew on the buttons and make a loose frill for the neck.

Waistcoat

1. Having cut out the relevant pattern pieces, sew the back and the back lining together at the neck. Turn and press.
2. Sew each front to a front lining at the neck, down the front and around the point to the side seams. Turn and press.
3. Sew the back and the fronts together at the shoulders.

4. Sew the side seams.
5. Tuck in the raw edges at the lower edge of the back and the back lining and sew.
6. Bind the armholes with contrasting binding.
7. Make the buttonholes and sew on the buttons.
8. Decorate one waistcoat front with hearts and the other with diamonds cut from a suitable contrasting fabric.

Shirts (see dia. 22, a-d)

BLINKY/SHORTY (a)

1. Having cut out the relevant pattern pieces, sew the front and the backs of the shirt together at the shoulders.
2. Fold and press the back opening to the inside. Hem neatly and sew on the press studs.
3. Make a narrow hem around the neck.
4. Make a narrow hem at the lower edge of the sleeves.
5. Stretch and sew elastic to gather the sleeves.
6. Gather the curved edge of the sleeve to fit the armhole. Sew into place.
7. Sew the underarm and side seams. Hem the bottom of the shirt.

CHARLIE AND AMADEUS (b)

1. Having cut out the relevant pattern pieces, sew the fronts and back of the shirt together at the shoulders.
2. Fold the collar along the fold line and stitch at each end (see dia. 22c) Turn to the right side and press. The collar may be omitted for Charlie and the neck left raggedy.
3. With right sides together, fold self-facing onto shirt fronts and sew the neck edge. Turn and press (see dia. 22d)
4. With right sides together, sew one section of the raw edge of the collar to the neck of the shirt. Fold in the raw edge of the other section of the collar and hand sew to the neck on the wrong side.
5. Make the buttonholes and sew on the buttons for Amadeus. Use safety pins for Charlie.
6. Gather the sleeves to fit the armholes. Sew into place.
7. Hem the lower edge of the sleeves which can be cut raggedy for Charlie.
8. Sew the underarm and side seams.
9. Hem the lower edge of the shirt.

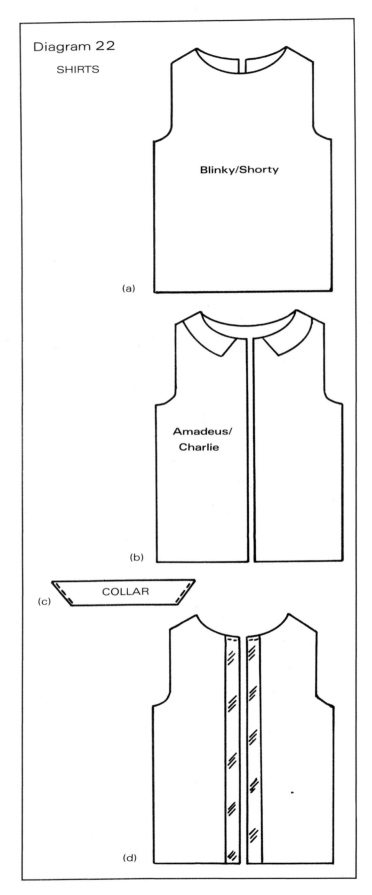

Diagram 22
SHIRTS

(a) Blinky/Shorty

(b) Amadeus/ Charlie

(c) COLLAR

(d)

Bow ties *(may be cut to any suitable size)*

1. Cut two pieces of fabric each 22 cm × 10 cm.
2. Sew the two pieces together right round, leaving a small section open. Turn, press and sew closed.
3. Cut a piece of fabric 2 cm × 5 cm. Fold in half lengthwise and sew down the long side. Turn to the right side and press with the seam at the back.
4. Wrap tightly around the centre of the tie to form a bow. Stitch into place by hand. Tack the bow to the front of the doll's neck.

Tie

1. Sew right round the tie, leaving the top open. Turn and press.
2. Fold in the raw edge and sew closed.
3. Cut a piece of fabric 6 cm × 7 cm. Fold lengthwise and sew down the long side. Turn and press with the seam at the back.
4. Fold this strip around the top of the tie to form a mock knot.
5. Tack the tie to the front of the doll's neck.

Hats

A large variety of straw and party hats is available at departmental stores, making it very easy to find a suitable hat for a clown. Or make one yourself from felt or fabric.

CONE HAT

1. Cut out the hat, following the instructions on the pattern.
2. Iron on a vilene lining on the wrong side.
3. With right side together, fold in half and sew from A to B and bind the lower edge. Add a pom-pom.

GLITZY HAT

1. Measure around the clown's head at the hairline to get the correct measurement for your doll as the hat must fit firmly. It should be about 40 cm.
2. Cut a 40 cm piece of fabric, adjust to suit your clown, by about 15 cm.
3. Trim one long edge with lace.
4. Fold in half and sew the two short edges together.
5. Gather the lace-trimmed edge and pull the gathers tightly.
6. Sew the hat to the doll's head by hand, turning in the raw edge at the same time.

JELLY BAG (see dia. 23)

1. Cut out the jelly bag as instructed on the diagram.

2. With right side facing, fold in half and sew along the two sides from A to B and bind the lower edge. Add a pom-pom.

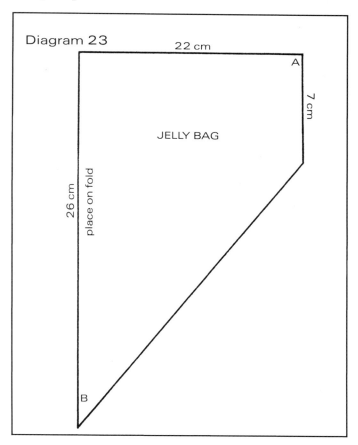

Diagram 23

22 cm

A

7 cm

JELLY BAG

26 cm

place on fold

B

TOP HAT

1. Cut the brim, side crown and top crown from both cardboard and felt, following the instructions on the pattern.
2. Sew the two pieces of felt brim together around the outer edge. Turn and press.
3. Place the cardboard brim inside the felt brim by overlapping the slit edges. Once the cardboard brim is inside the felt brim, mend the slit with sticky tape. Hand sew the brim closed.
4. Sew the short (felt) sides of the crown together to form a tube. Turn to the right side. Glue the matching cardboard sides together. Place the felt tube over the cardboard tube. Fold in the excess at the top and bottom and glue on the inside.

5. Place the felt crown over the cardboard crown. Fold the excess to the inside and glue.
6. Sew the crown to the top and the brim to the bottom of the tube by hand. Trim.

SUNHAT (see dia. 24)

1. Cut the crown of the hat, using a plate approximately 24 cm in diameter.
2. Use iron-on Vilene to stiffen the brim (optional).
3. Sew the short sides of the brim together to form a circle. Repeat for the lining.
4. Place the brim and the lining together and sew right round the outer edge. Turn and press.
5. Gather the crown to fit the brim. Place the gathered edge of the crown between the brim and the lining and, folding in the raw edge, sew the crown to the brim.

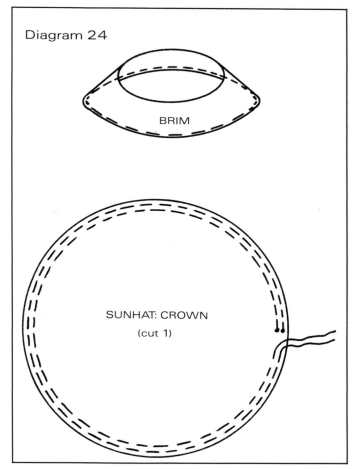

Diagram 24

BRIM

SUNHAT: CROWN

(cut 1)

ACCESSORIES
∙∙∙

Rabbit

1. Cut out the rabbit following the instructions on the pattern.
2. Sew right round, leaving a small opening for stuffing. Turn to the right side.
3. Stuff lightly and sew closed.
4. Cut out the eyes and the nose from felt and glue in position.
5. Draw a simple mouth and a few lashes.
6. Put powdered blusher on the cheeks and tie a bow around the neck.

Cigarette

1. Cut a strip of white or cream fabric about 2 cm × 6 cm.
2. Cover one entire side of the fabric with glue and roll up with the glue to the inside to form the cigarette.
3. Dip one end into red paint. Before the paint dries, add a wisp of stuffing for the smoke.
4. As Charlie is ornamental, the cigarette is held in place with a pin.

Braces

1. Using vinyl, cut three 'clips' for the braces from the pattern.
2. Cut two straps each about 20 cm long from ribbon or felt.
3. Sew one vinyl 'clip' to one end of each strap and the third to the other ends of the straps, which must be sewn together to form a Y-shaped pair of braces.

Beads

1. Blinky's winking eye, Charlie's tears and Floppy's stars are beads which have been glued in position.
2. Sequins and beads were used to decorate the frills and shoes of the glitzy Floppy.

Pom-poms

Plastic kits which enable you to make a variety of pom-poms in minutes are available from craft shops.

Buttons

Any brightly coloured buttons may be used. The buttons seen on these clowns were bought at a craft market and are made from self-hardening clay.

Shoes and socks

1. Trim the shoe uppers as shown in dia. 25. Adding a contrasting toe cap will also add variety. Sewing on the soles with the wrong sides together will make the shoes look both different and larger.
2. The tennis shoes were bought from the baby section of a departmental store and are a size 2. If you would like the clown to have bigger feet, buy larger shoes and stuff the toes.
3. The clowns with tennis shoes are wearing baby socks, size 3-6 months. Where the shoes form part of the doll, the socks can either be omitted or mock socks can be made by sewing rib trim around the legs.

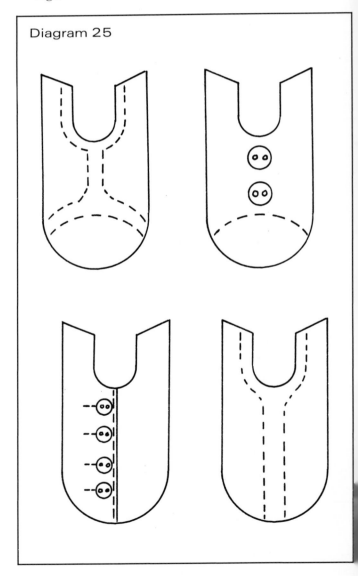

Diagram 25

Cane ring

1. Bend a piece of cane about 50 cm long into a circle.
2. Secure with a staple or tape and paint.

Hoops

The hoops held by Puddystix are children's plastic bangles.

Frills *(see dia. 26)*

1. Frills can be made to any suitable size required. See the instructions as given for Floppy on p. 17.
2. Blinky also has an optional frill down the front of his shirt. Cut one strip of fabric 8 cm × 18 cm, and another 4 cm × 18 cm. Make a narrow hem right round each strip. Place the wrong side of the narrow strip on top of the right side of the wide strip and gather the two strips together along the centre. Pull up gathers until frill measures 13 cm. Sew to the front of the shirt.

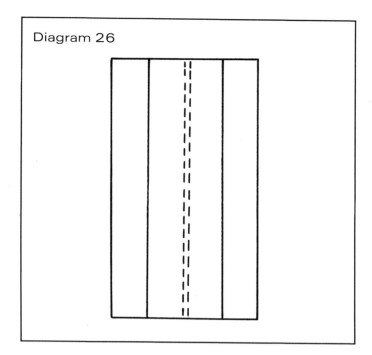

Diagram 26

PATTERNS

...

FACES FOR **Puddystix**

Eye positions

Nose position

Mouth position

Try designing your own clown face here

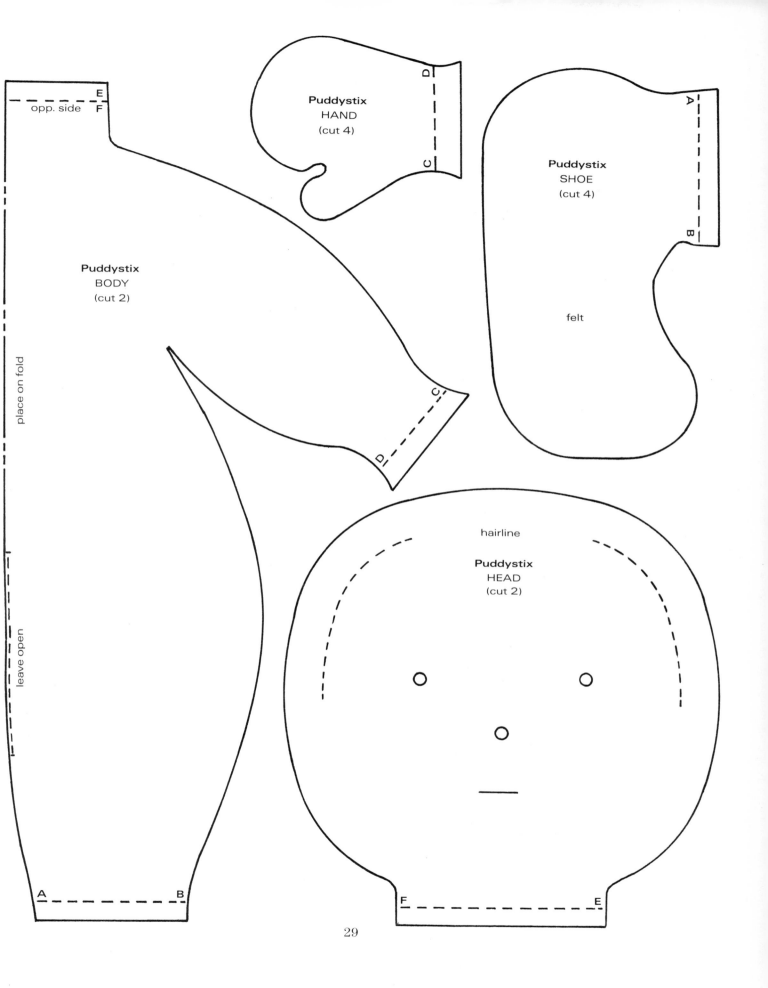

Puddystix
HAND
(cut 4)

Puddystix
SHOE
(cut 4)

felt

E
opp. side F

Puddystix
BODY
(cut 2)

place on fold

leave open

A   B

D
C

C
D

hairline

Puddystix
HEAD
(cut 2)

F   E

29

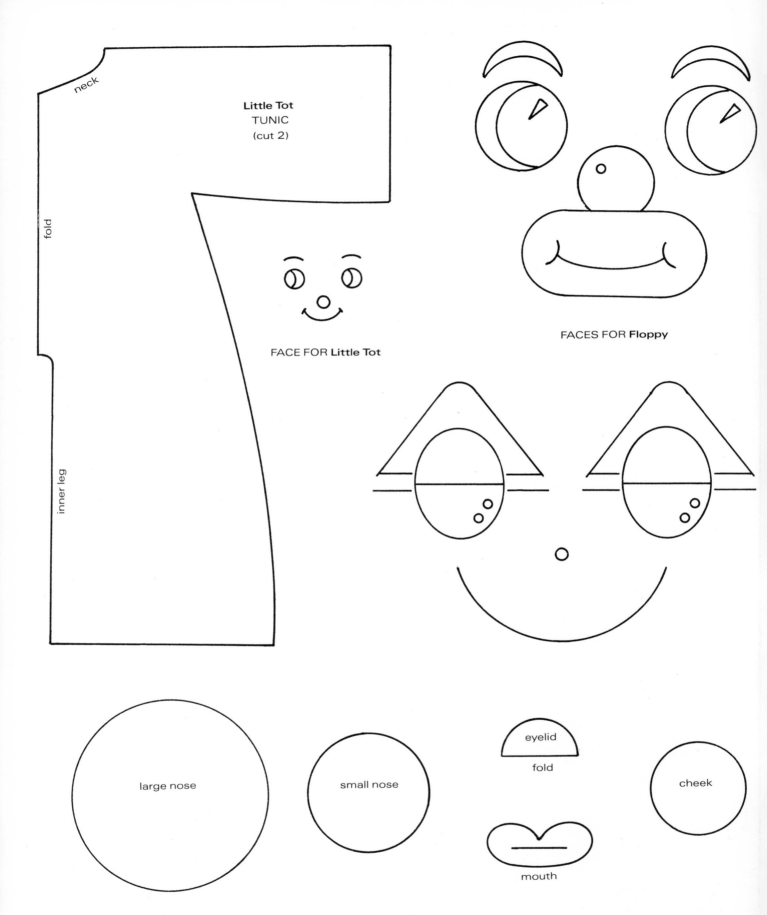

Little Tot
TUNIC
(cut 2)

neck

fold

inner leg

FACE FOR **Little Tot**

FACES FOR **Floppy**

large nose

small nose

eyelid

fold

cheek

mouth

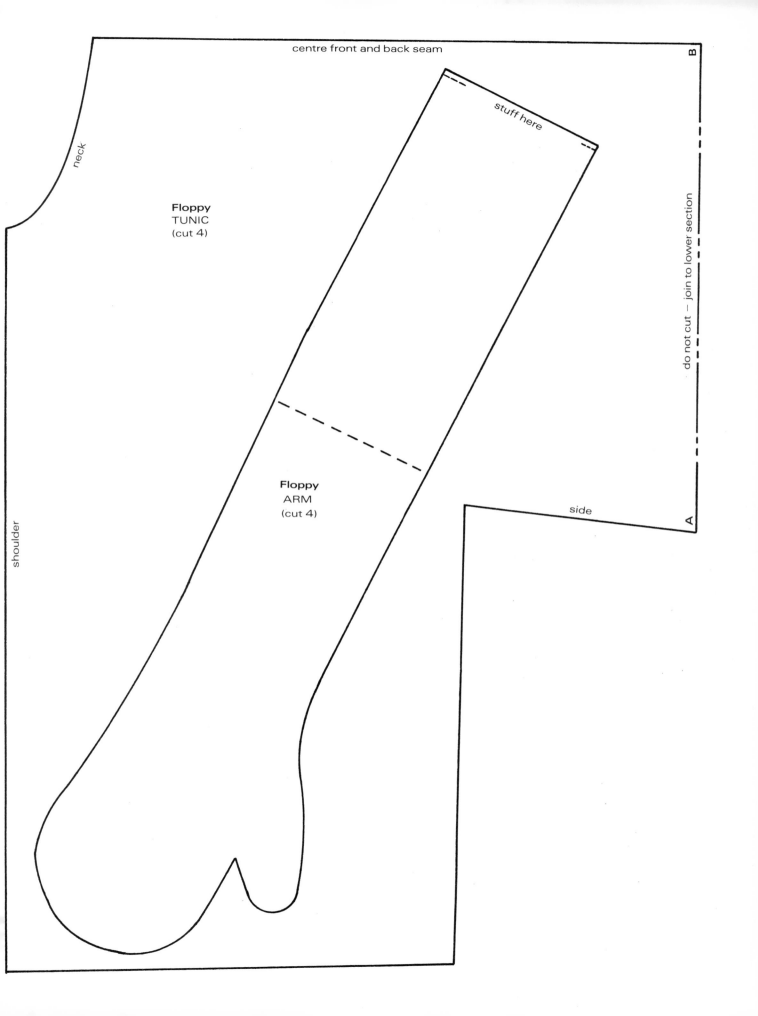

centre front and back seam

neck

Floppy
TUNIC
(cut 4)

stuff here

B

do not cut – join to lower section

Floppy
ARM
(cut 4)

side

A

shoulder

centre front and back seam

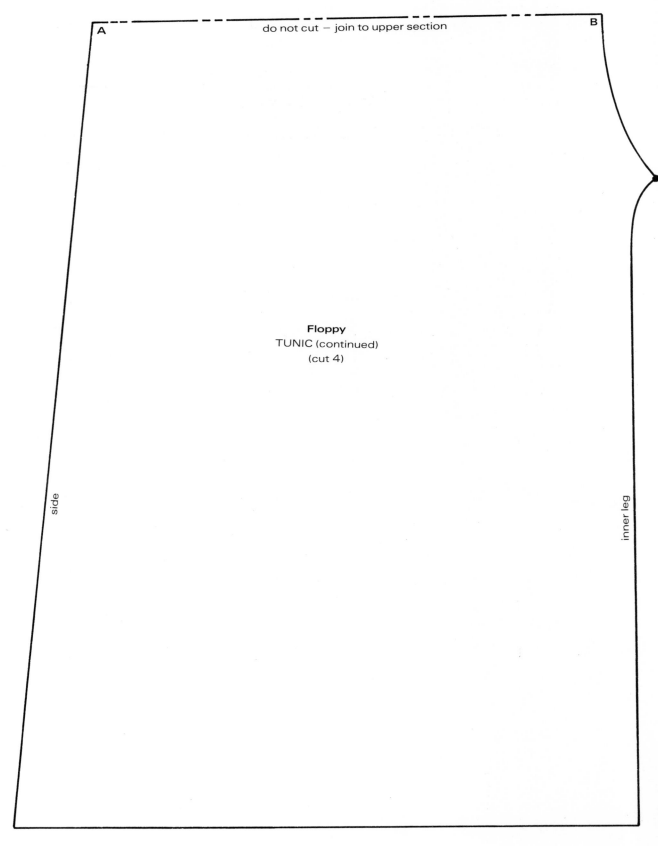

A

do not cut – join to upper section

B

Floppy
TUNIC (continued)
(cut 4)

side

inner leg

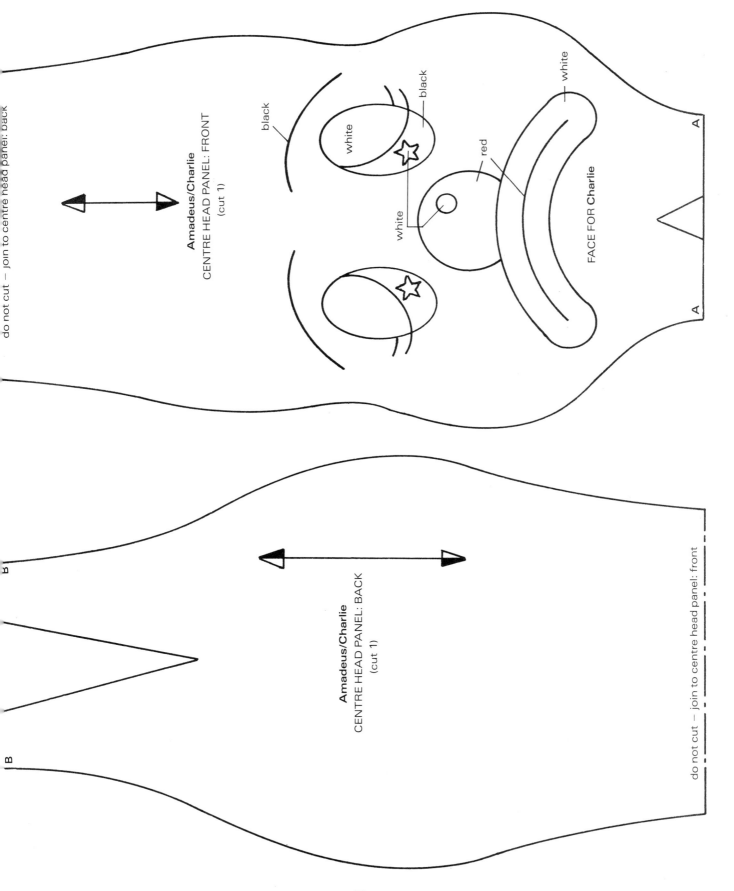

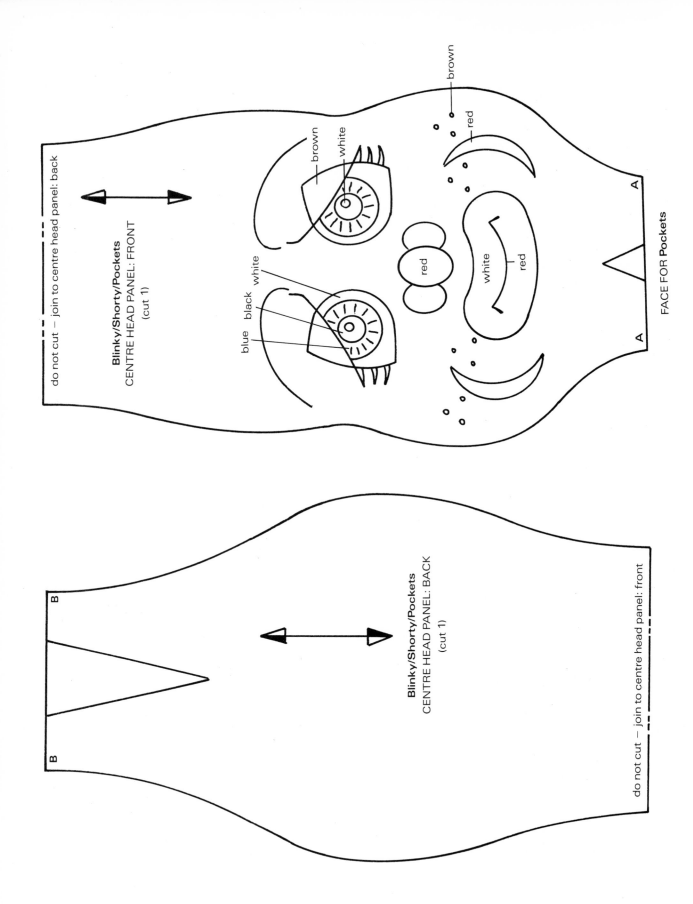

do not cut – join to centre head panel: back

Blinky/Shorty/Pockets
CENTRE HEAD PANEL: FRONT
(cut 1)

brown

white

white

black

blue

red

white

red

brown

red

A

A

FACE FOR **Pockets**

B

B

Blinky/Shorty/Pockets
CENTRE HEAD PANEL: BACK
(cut 1)

do not cut – join to centre head panel: front

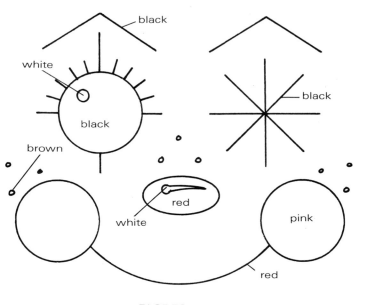

FACE FOR **Blinky**

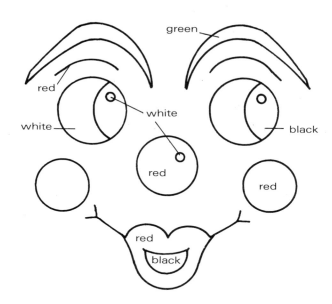

FACE FOR **Shorty**

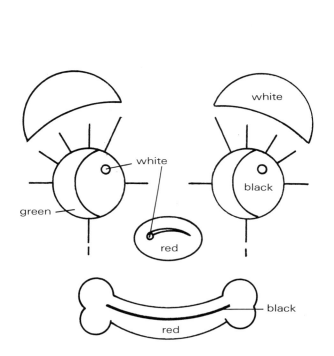

FACE FOR **Shorty**

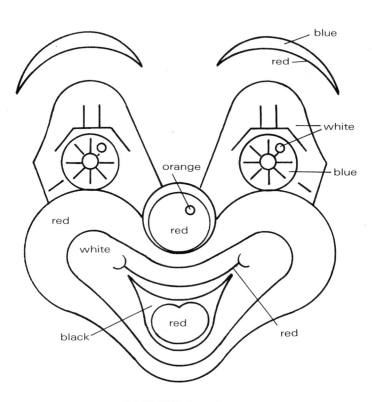

FACE FOR **Amadeus**

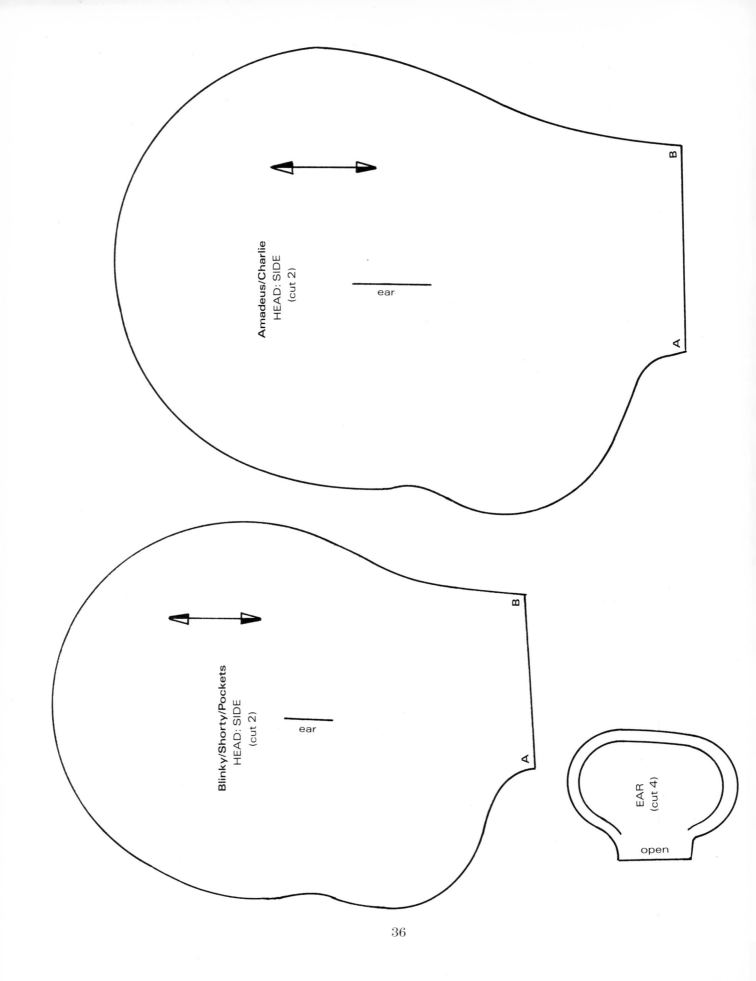

Amadeus/Charlie
HEAD: SIDE
(cut 2)

ear

B

A

Blinky/Shorty/Pockets
HEAD: SIDE
(cut 2)

ear

B

A

EAR
(cut 4)

open

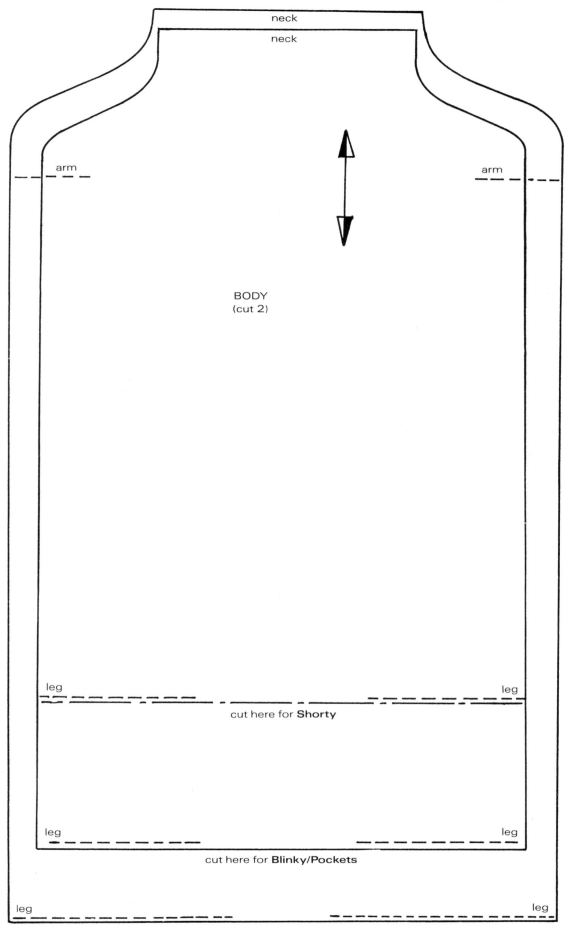

neck

neck

arm

arm

BODY
(cut 2)

leg

leg

cut here for **Shorty**

leg

leg

cut here for **Blinky/Pockets**

leg

leg

cut here for **Amadeus/Charlie**

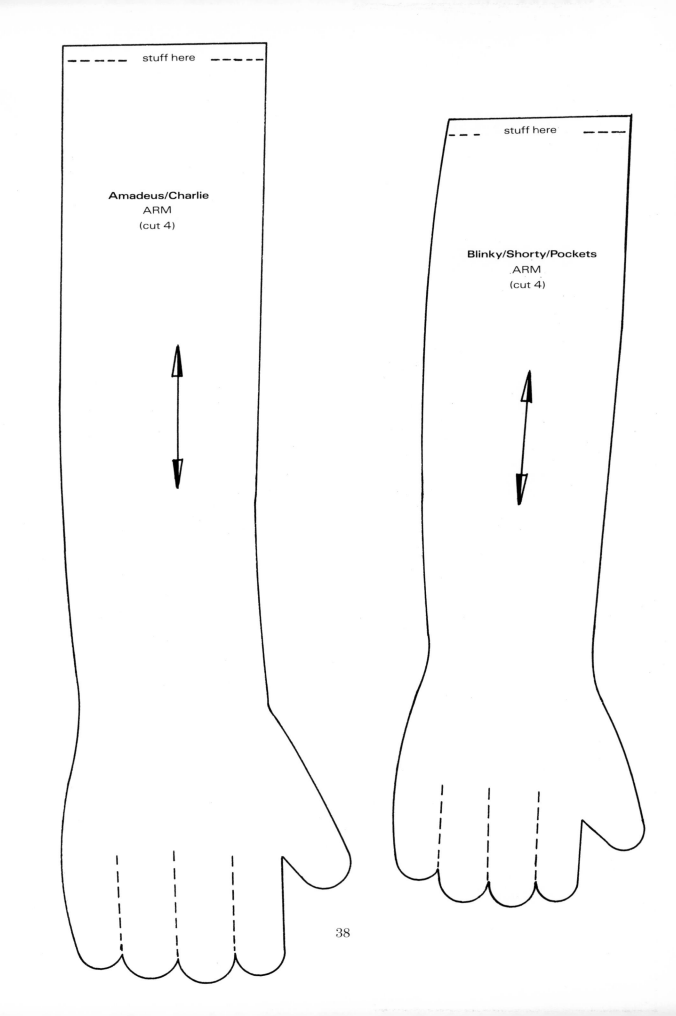

stuff here

Amadeus/Charlie
ARM
(cut 4)

stuff here

Blinky/Shorty/Pockets
ARM
(cut 4)

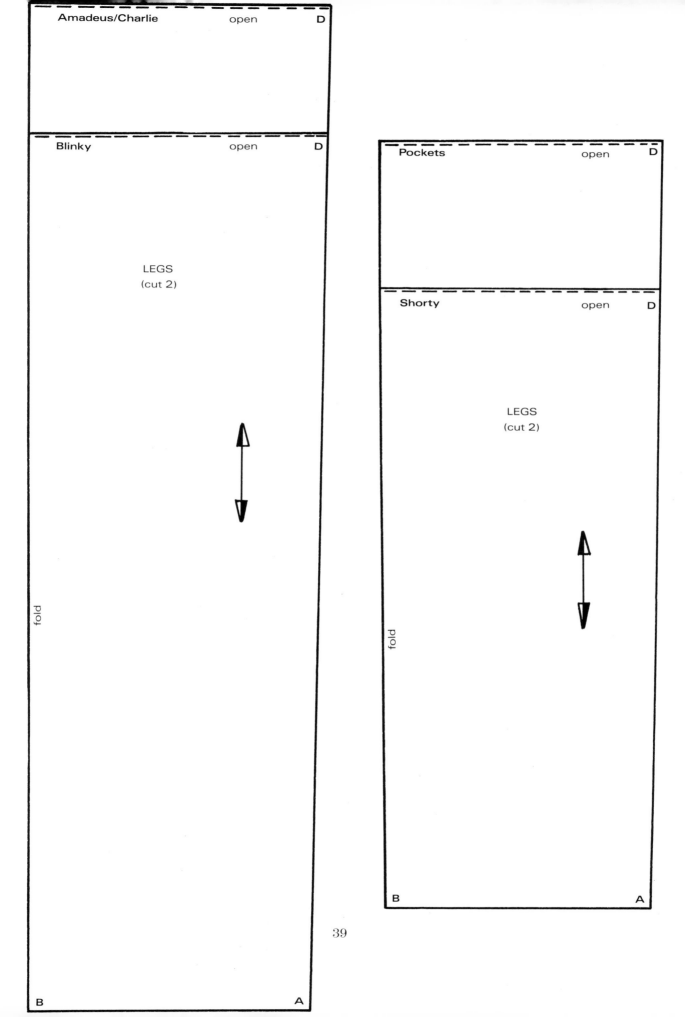

Amadeus/Charlie   open   D

B   A

Blinky   open   D

LEGS
(cut 2)

fold

Pockets   open   D

Shorty   open   D

LEGS
(cut 2)

fold

B   A

39

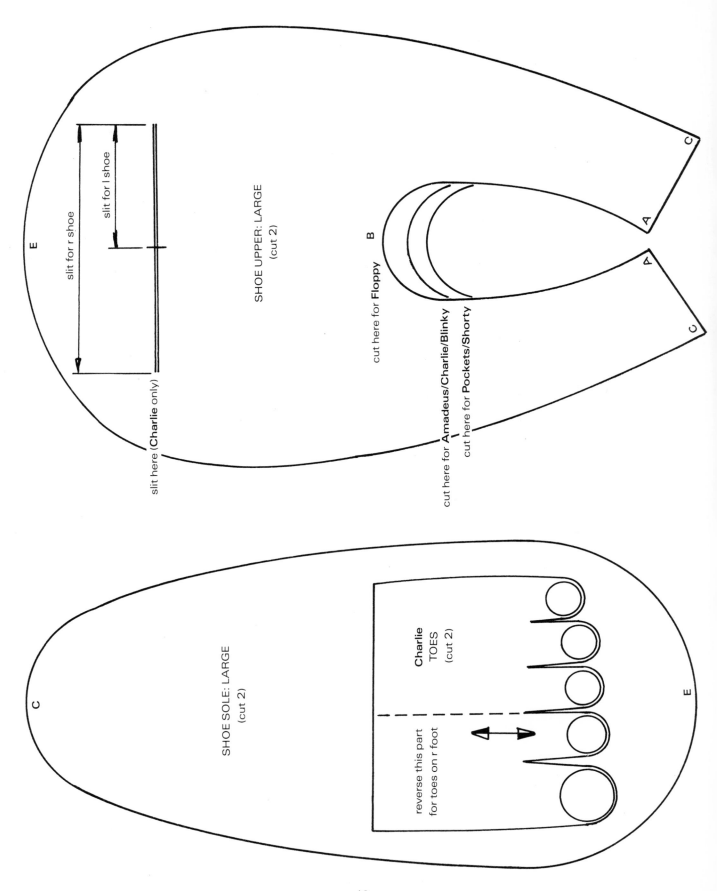

slit for r shoe

slit for l shoe

E

slit here (**Charlie** only)

SHOE UPPER: LARGE
(cut 2)

B

cut here for **Floppy**

cut here for **Amadeus/Charlie/Blinky**

cut here for **Pockets/Shorty**

C

A

A

C

SHOE SOLE: LARGE
(cut 2)

C

E

Charlie
TOES
(cut 2)

reverse this part
for toes on r foot

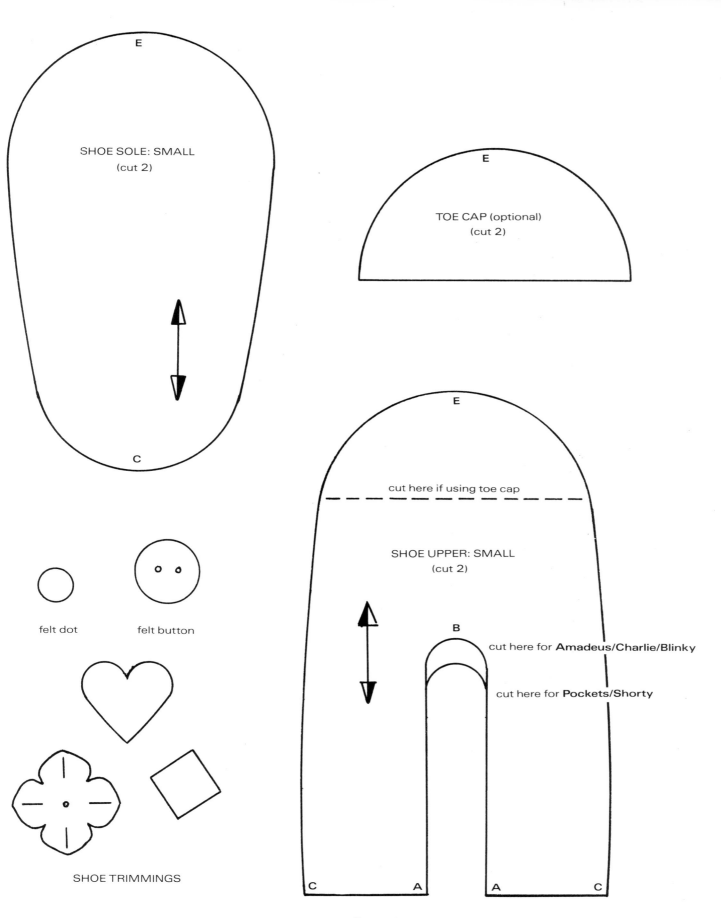

SHOE SOLE: SMALL
(cut 2)

E

C

TOE CAP (optional)
(cut 2)

E

felt dot

felt button

SHOE TRIMMINGS

SHOE UPPER: SMALL
(cut 2)

E

cut here if using toe cap

B

cut here for **Amadeus/Charlie/Blinky**

cut here for **Pockets/Shorty**

C   A   A   C

41

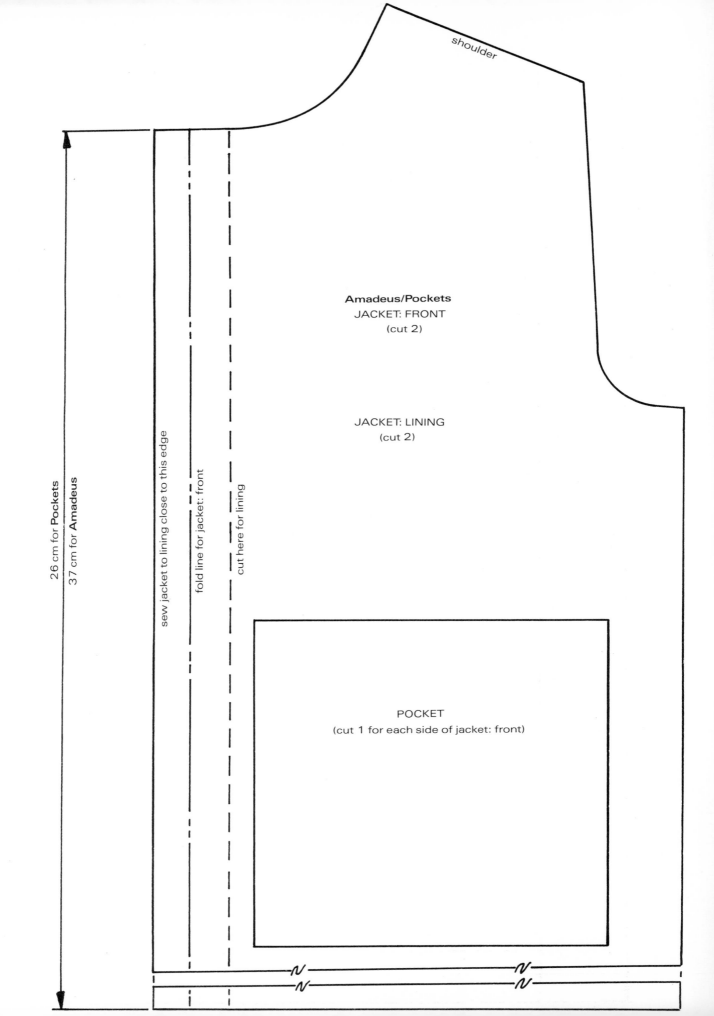

Amadeus/Pockets
JACKET: FRONT
(cut 2)

JACKET: LINING
(cut 2)

POCKET
(cut 1 for each side of jacket: front)

shoulder

26 cm for **Pockets**

37 cm for **Amadeus**

sew jacket to lining close to this edge

fold line for jacket: front

cut here for lining

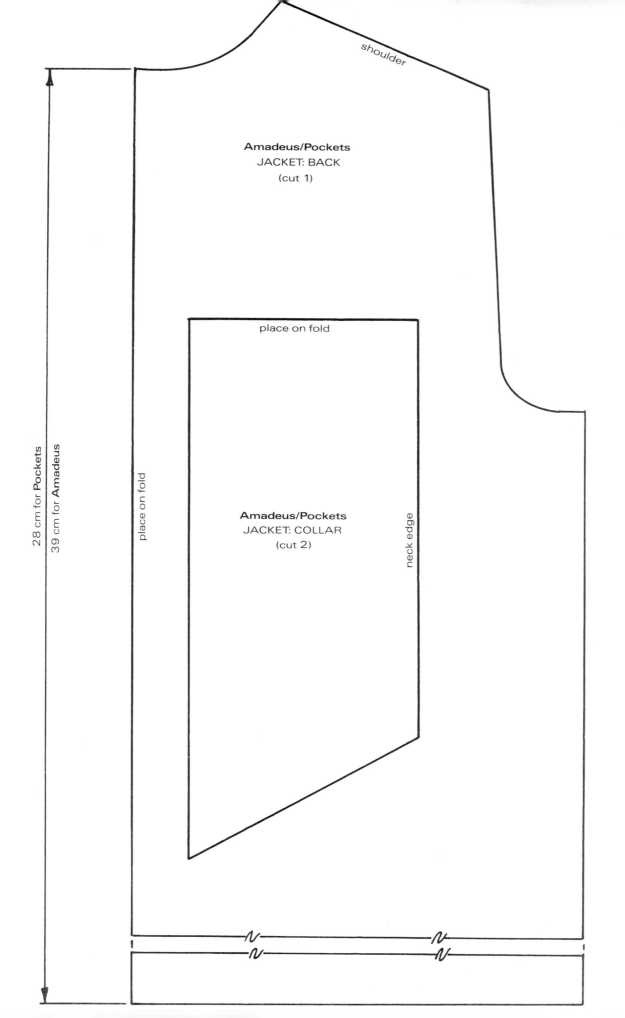

shoulder

Amadeus/Pockets
JACKET: BACK
(cut 1)

place on fold

Amadeus/Pockets
JACKET: COLLAR
(cut 2)

neck edge

place on fold

28 cm for **Pockets**

39 cm for **Amadeus**

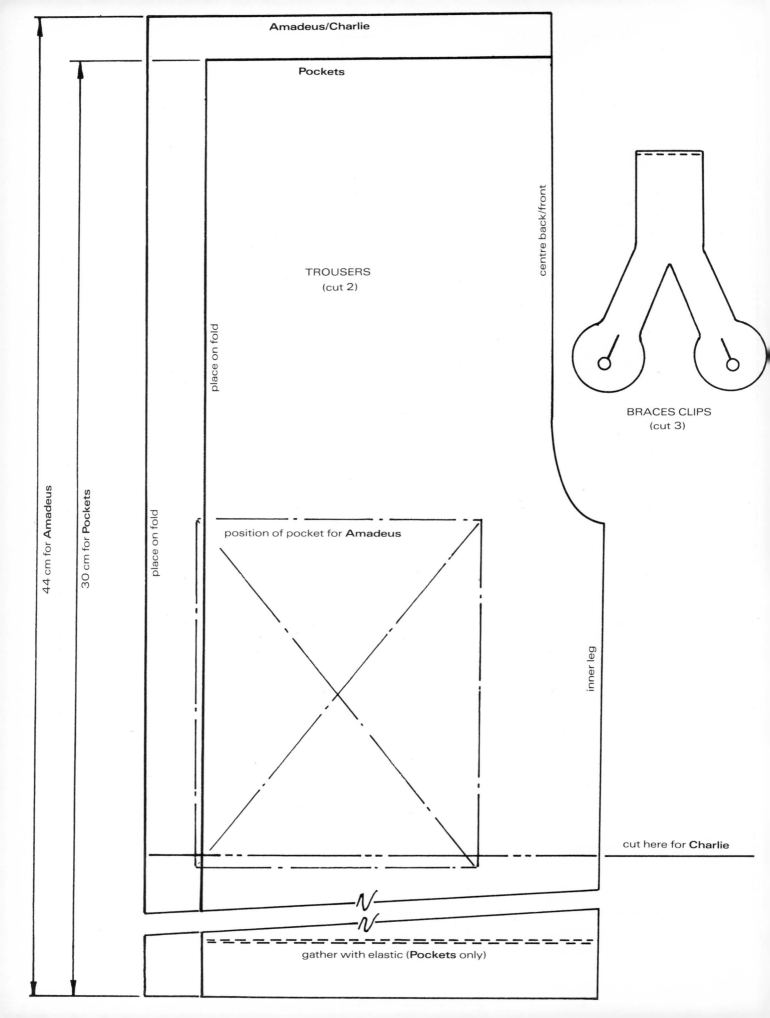

Amadeus/Charlie

Pockets

TROUSERS
(cut 2)

centre back/front

place on fold

place on fold

44 cm for **Amadeus**

30 cm for **Pockets**

position of pocket for **Amadeus**

inner leg

BRACES CLIPS
(cut 3)

cut here for **Charlie**

gather with elastic (**Pockets** only)

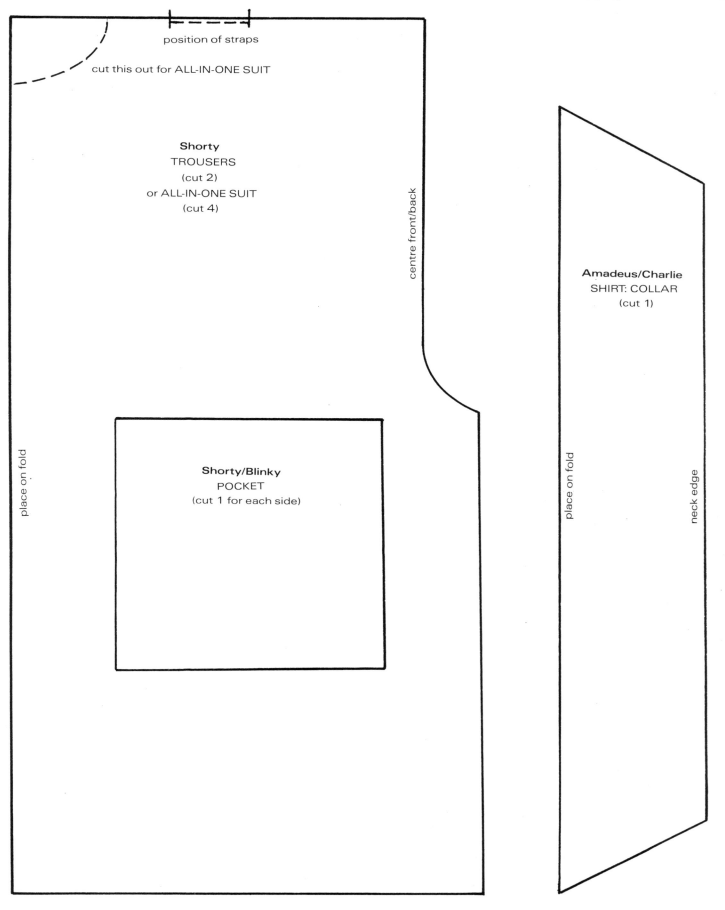

position of straps

cut this out for ALL-IN-ONE SUIT

Shorty
TROUSERS
(cut 2)
or ALL-IN-ONE SUIT
(cut 4)

centre front/back

Amadeus/Charlie
SHIRT: COLLAR
(cut 1)

Shorty/Blinky
POCKET
(cut 1 for each side)

place on fold

place on fold

neck edge

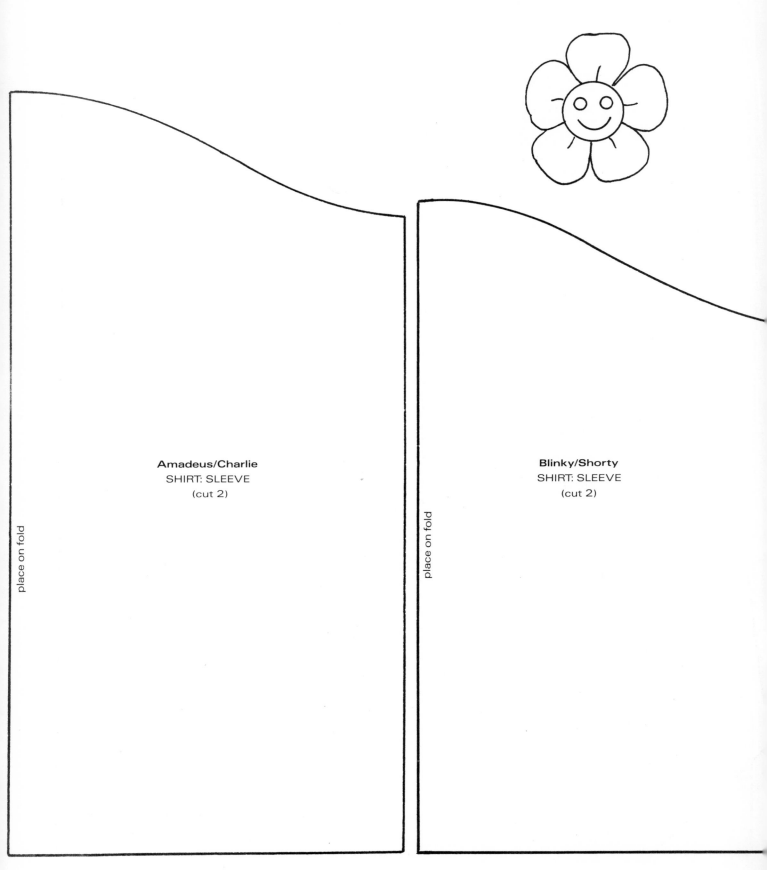

place on fold

Amadeus/Charlie
SHIRT: SLEEVE
(cut 2)

place on fold

Blinky/Shorty
SHIRT: SLEEVE
(cut 2)

46

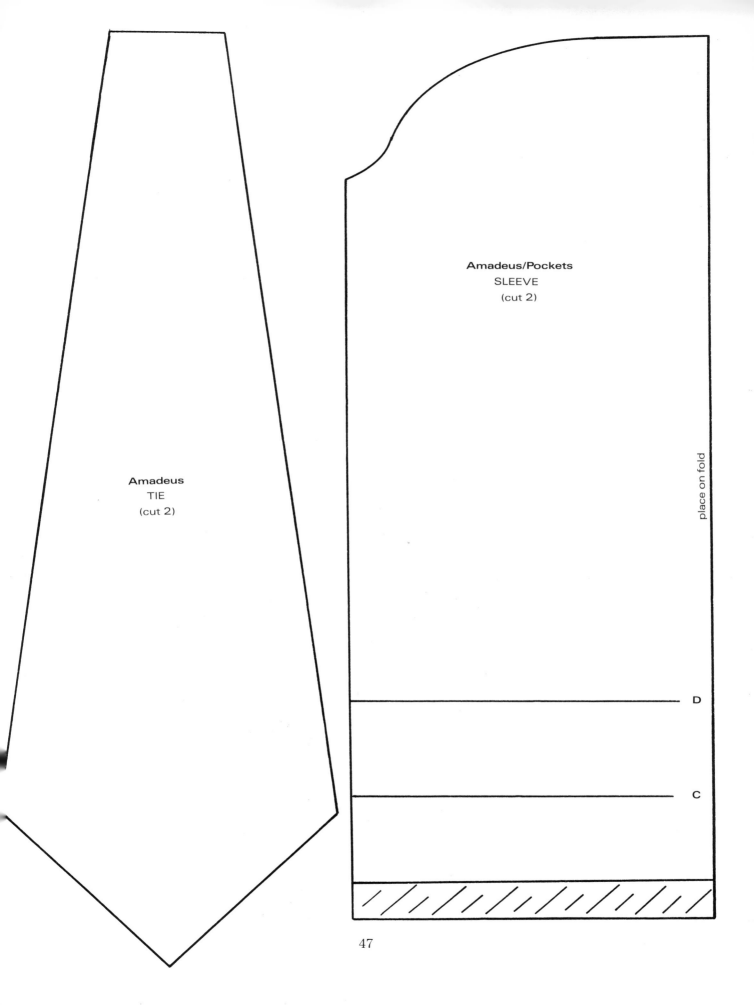

Amadeus
TIE
(cut 2)

Amadeus/Pockets
SLEEVE
(cut 2)

place on fold

D

C

47

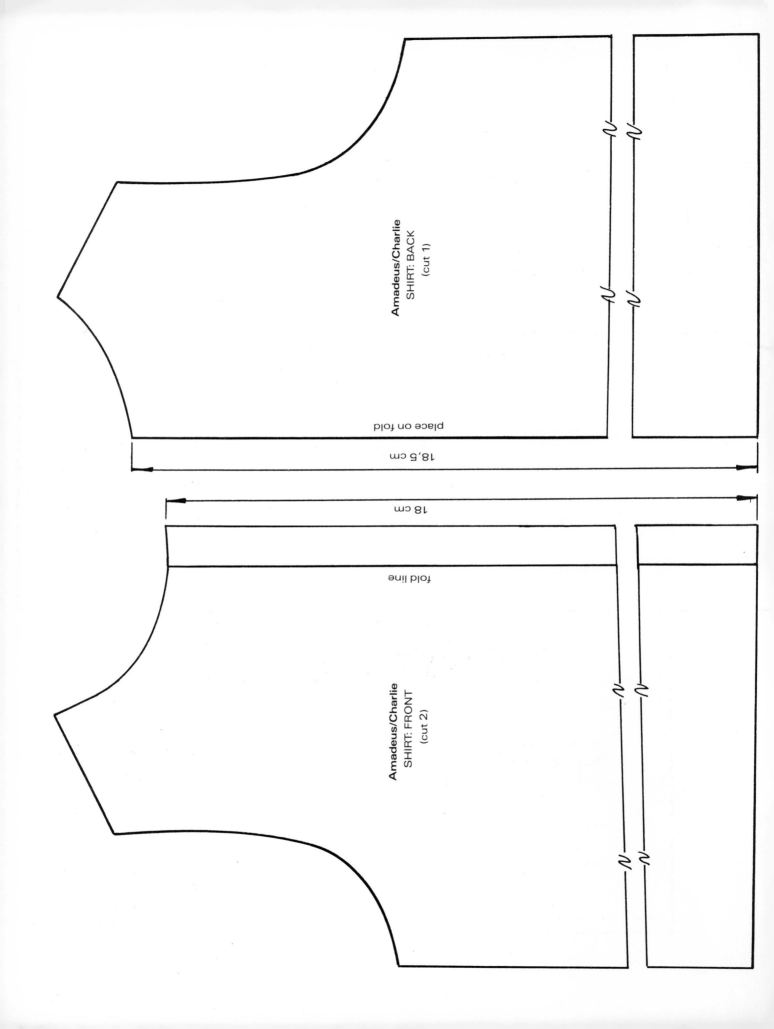

Amadeus/Charlie
SHIRT: BACK
(cut 1)

place on fold

18,5 cm

18 cm

fold line

Amadeus/Charlie
SHIRT: FRONT
(cut 2)

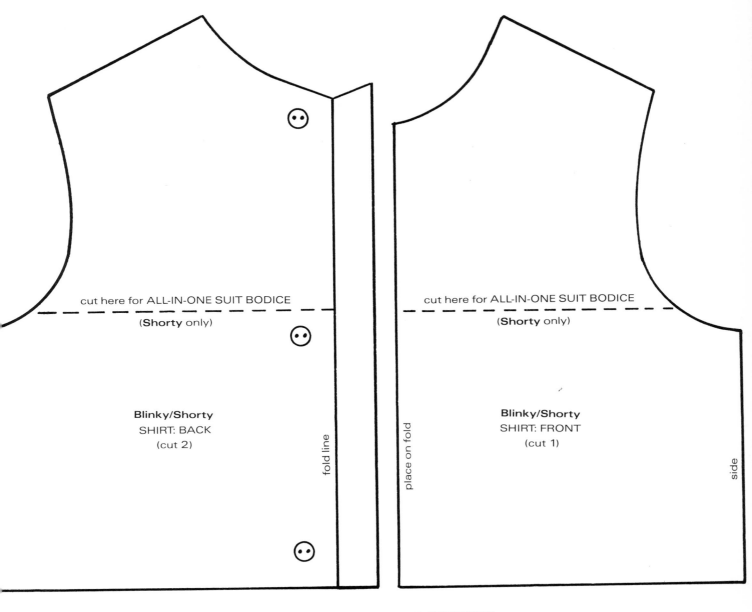

cut here for ALL-IN-ONE SUIT BODICE

(**Shorty** only)

cut here for ALL-IN-ONE SUIT BODICE

(**Shorty** only)

Blinky/Shorty
SHIRT: BACK
(cut 2)

fold line

place on fold

Blinky/Shorty
SHIRT: FRONT
(cut 1)

side

Amadeus
POCKET

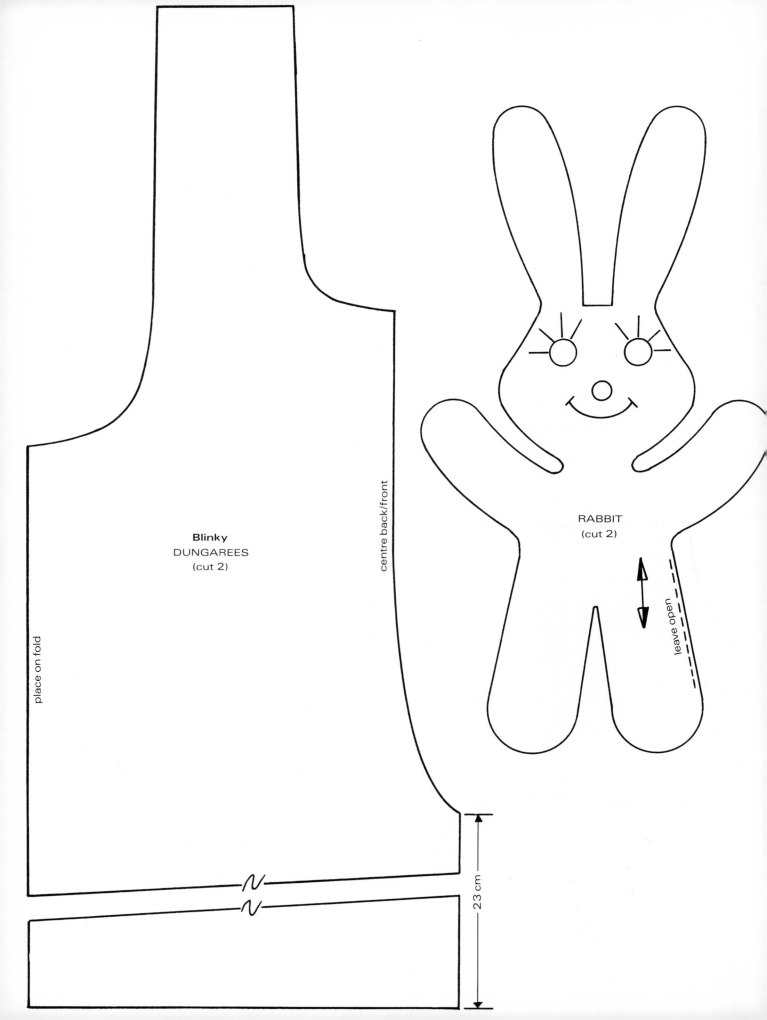

Blinky
DUNGAREES
(cut 2)

place on fold

centre back/front

23 cm

RABBIT
(cut 2)

leave open

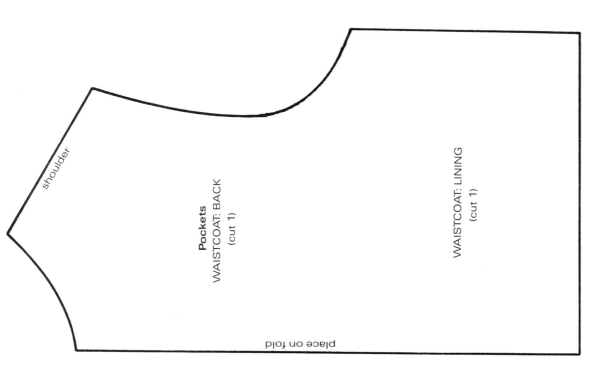

shoulder

Pockets
WAISTCOAT: BACK
(cut 1)

WAISTCOAT: LINING
(cut 1)

place on fold

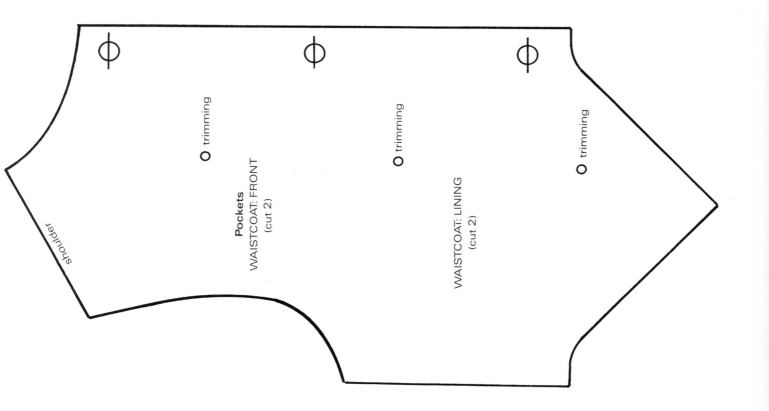

shoulder

trimming

trimming

trimming

Pockets
WAISTCOAT: FRONT
(cut 2)

WAISTCOAT: LINING
(cut 2)

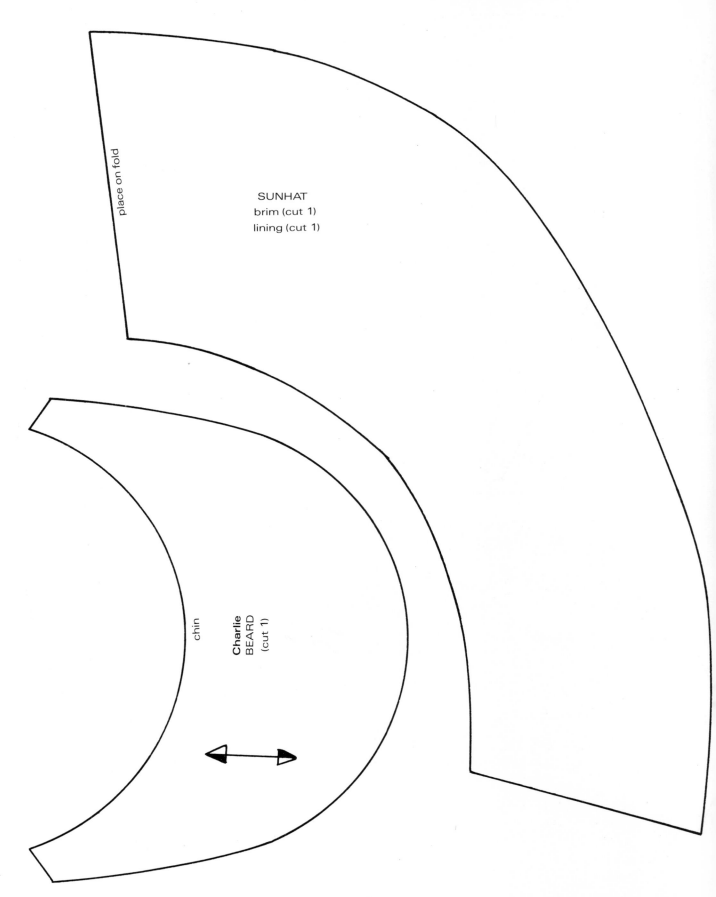

place on fold

SUNHAT
brim (cut 1)
lining (cut 1)

chin

Charlie
BEARD
(cut 1)

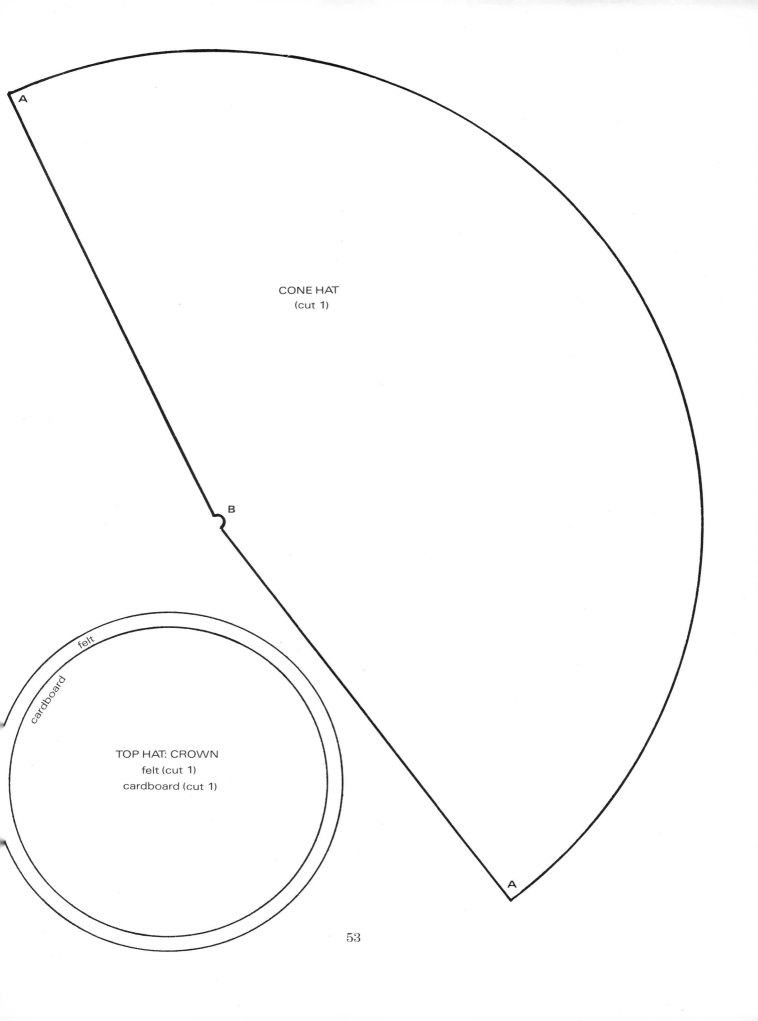

CONE HAT
(cut 1)

A

B

A

felt

cardboard

TOP HAT: CROWN
felt (cut 1)
cardboard (cut 1)

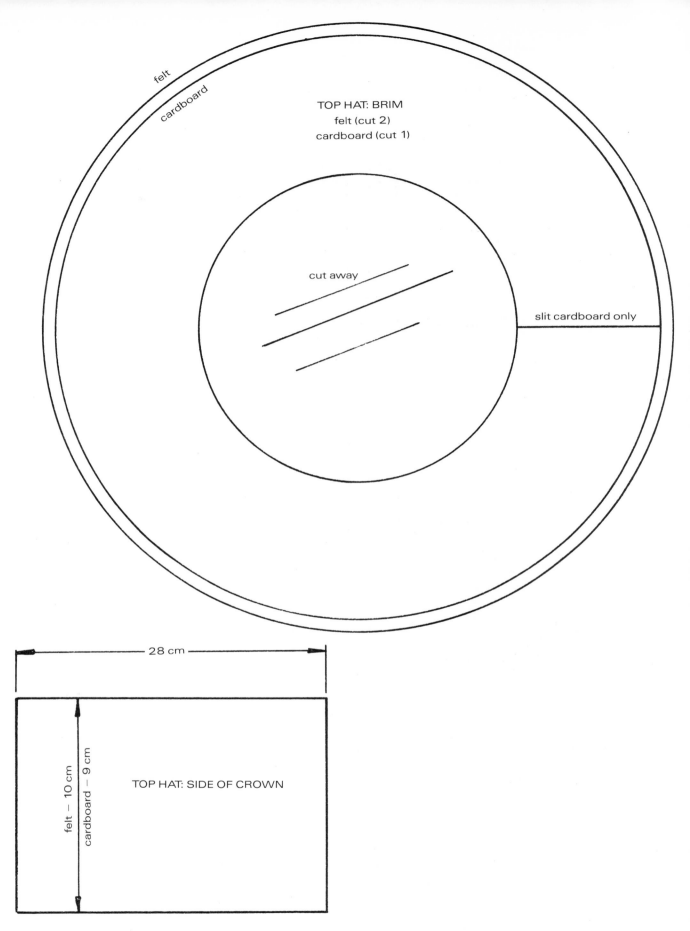

felt

cardboard

TOP HAT: BRIM
felt (cut 2)
cardboard (cut 1)

cut away

slit cardboard only

← 28 cm →

felt – 10 cm
cardboard – 9 cm

TOP HAT: SIDE OF CROWN

THE DOLL STAND

The diagram for the doll stand is self-explanatory.

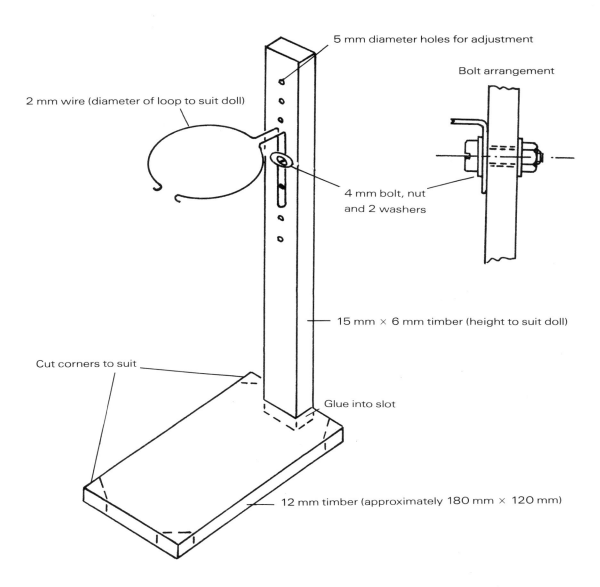

5 mm diameter holes for adjustment

Bolt arrangement

2 mm wire (diameter of loop to suit doll)

4 mm bolt, nut and 2 washers

15 mm × 6 mm timber (height to suit doll)

Cut corners to suit

Glue into slot

12 mm timber (approximately 180 mm × 120 mm)

Buyer's guide

Many of the supplies needed to make
cloth clowns and cloth dolls are available
from Nod Dolls, P.O. Box 73422, Fairland 2030.
Please send a long, self-addressed, stamped envelope
to the above address for more information
and a free catalogue.